1992

Management Research

Management Research
An Introduction

Mark Easterby-Smith
Richard Thorpe
Andy Lowe

SAGE Publications
London • Newbury Park • New Delhi

SAGE Publications Ltd
6 Bonhill Street
London EC2A 4PU

SAGE Publications Inc
2455 Teller Road
Newbury Park, California 91320

SAGE Publications India Pvt Ltd
32, M-Block Market
Greater Kailash – I
New Delhi 110 048

British Library Cataloguing in Publication Data

Easterby-Smith, Mark
    Management research: An introduction.
    I. Title   II. Thorpe, Richard   III. Lowe, Andy
    650.07

    ISBN 0–8039–8392–1
    ISBN 0–8039–8393–X pbk

Library of Congress catalog card number 91–052835

Typeset by Mayhew Typesetting, Bristol, England
Printed in Great Britain by Dotesios Ltd, Trowbridge, Wiltshire

658.0072
E131

Contents

142,947

Contents

About the Authors

Mark Easterby-Smith is Director of the Management Teacher
Development Centre at Lancaster University and a Senior Lecturer in
the Department of Management Learning. He has a first degree in
engineering science and a PhD in organisation behaviour. During the
1970s he was involved in evaluation of management development
programmes and systems at Durham University Business School. This
and continuing research has led to three books, *Management
Development in the Organisation* (Macmillan), *Auditing Management
Development* (Gower), and *Evaluation of Management Education,
Training and Development* (Gower).

From 1980–4 he was director of the postgraduate research
programme in the Department of Management Learning, and from
1980–7 he was editor of *Management Education and Development*, the
journal of the Association for Management Education and
Development.

More recently, following involvement in the Faculty of the
International Teachers Programme, he has developed national and
European programmes for new teachers in management. These
programmes are being supported by substantial funding from the
Economic and Social Research Council (ESRC) and the Foundation
for Management Education (FME).

Richard Thorpe is a Principal Lecturer in Management Development in
the Department of Management and Course Leader of the MBA
programme at Manchester Polytechnic. After spending a number of
years in industry, culminating in managing a manufacturing company
in the Highlands of Scotland, he joined Strathclyde University. There
as a research fellow he undertook a national study of incentive
payment schemes in Britain. This work led to collaboration in two
publications, *Incentive Schemes in Britain 1978–1980* (Department of
Employment) and *Payment Systems and Productivity* (Macmillan). In
1980 he joined Glasgow University where he continued to widen his
research experience and made regular contributions to the Scottish
Business Schools Doctoral Programme. In 1983 he attended the
International Teachers Programme in Sweden where he met Mark and
embarked on a PhD under Mark's supervision. The research related to
aspects of small and medium-sized company growth and development.
It was in grappling with issues of methodology that he met Andy
Lowe at Small Firm Policy and Research Conferences, and thus a link
between the writers was forged and from this link came the inspiration
for this book.

Richard is currently coordinator for research in the Department of Management at Manchester Polytechnic.

Andy Lowe is Lecturer in Marketing in the Department of Marketing at the University of Strathclyde, Glasgow. Following ten years in executive positions with companies in the United States and Britain Andy took an MBA at the University of Aston. Subsequently he was the marketing manager for a software company specialising in multi-user hotel systems, before beginning an academic career in Scotland. After a period at Robert Gordons Institute of Technology in Aberdeen he took up his current academic position at the University of Strathclyde where he teaches qualitative methodologies on the Scottish Business Schools Doctoral Programme and qualitative market research and the marketing of services to postgraduate students. His PhD from the University of Glasgow was an exploratory study of small business survival in Scottish rural hotels. He has been the academic adviser to the *Market Forces* series on BBC Radio Four. His current research interests are concerned with exploratory studies in marketing the Arts and marketing Professional Services. In addition to his academic career he owns a consultancy company, Creative Business Solutions.

Preface

Most people write books for two main reasons: to acquire fame (or notoriety), and to make money. We are no exception to this general principle; but in case we are not outrageously successful on either score we can offer some other reasons.

First of all we have written the book for the research community in management; for anyone who is actually doing some research, whether it be a student project, a doctoral thesis or a company-based investigation. Even experienced researchers still find the existing methodology literature to be of limited value in practice, and our message to the research community is that management research is both more complex and more simple than is normally implied by the textbooks. It is more complex in that, when you are conducting research into managing/managers/management, a number of factors beyond the technicalities of research design or the use of a particular method assume considerable importance. These start with the philosophical issues underlying management research, because the world view of the researcher can influence both the selection of methods and judgements about the quality and value of outcomes. Political issues are also important here because of the frequent need to gain access to organisations and to handle the dynamics of power within and between organisations.

On the other hand, research should be more simple because it needs to be appropriate to the task in hand, and not designed just to follow elaborate rules and procedures. It is largely about being able to compromise, to pose the right questions, and to answer them in a way that satisfies the majority of interested parties. It should also be concerned with developing deeper insights into the processes and techniques of management, but this often has to be conducted in parallel with the more pragmatic interests of researchers and those who help them.

Secondly, we have written for those on the receiving end of management research. They may be the clients of formal research projects, and the people who might benefit from, or be harmed by, the process and results of the research. For these people we hope to provide insights both into what management research is, and into what it can be. We also hope that the book will provide them with a basis for evaluating the quality of research designs in case they are in the business of commissioning projects that will be carried out by others.

Thirdly, we have written the book for ourselves. Writing provides an excellent discipline for clarifying one's ideas, and a stimulus for exploring new areas. We have also found it a considerable challenge to work together on the production of the book. We have brought to the venture some very different experiences, frameworks and personal styles. Indeed, the only things that we may genuinely have in common are an interest in climbing and a commitment to collaborative work. We suspect that the diversity represented by the three authors will be seen both as the strength and the weakness of the book. The task of knitting together these different styles into a reasonably coherent whole has, at times, not been easy. But we have also found that the challenges we have posed and the deadlines we have placed upon each other have been extremely stimulating. The opportunity to compare and exchange ideas through meetings and writing has, we believe, enabled us to develop our ideas considerably beyond their starting points. And in a way that is how we regard the book as a whole: not as a final statement on management research methods, but as one point reached in a journey of discovery. We hope that readers will use it in the same way.

Acknowledgements

This book is based on the personal research experience of the authors. However, thanks should also go to a number of colleagues who have contributed to the text both through their encouragement and through their ideas, which have to varying degrees been reflected in the text.

Worthy of particular note are Ardha Best, who helped us think through aspects of the qualitative methods chapter, Diane Philips, who helped at the drafting stages of our quantitative chapter, and Tim Stone, Kate Morrison and Jean Moscarola, who made other useful contributions. Also Jean Claude Usunier provided a valuable critique of the whole book from a European perspective.

Perhaps the most important critic of our work has been Sue Jones, our editor from Sage. Her comments were always useful and direct and have enabled us to sharpen our thinking in a great many areas.

Over the last few months, as the book reached its final stages, the bulk of the typing and coordination work has fallen to Caroline Berresford, to whom we are most grateful for her patience and continuing enthusiasm. We would also like to thank Herbert Thorpe for his assistance in reading the proofs.

Finally, we would like to thank our families for their tolerance whilst this book was being written – we hope they will find it was worth the effort.

PART ONE
Starting Management Research

1
Introducing Management Research

This book is written for people who are doing research into management, possibly for the first time, where their research involves collecting and interpreting information and deciding what to do with it. It is also intended for experienced people who wish to tackle new kinds of research problems or methods, and who are aware of the lack of literature providing both theoretical and practical guidance.

Our aim is to draw together the main threads of management research and to provide a bridge between theoretical and practical issues. This inevitably involves much selectivity, and we feel it is only fair to start by sharing some of our assumptions about management and research. Firstly, we do not see management research as being the exclusive preserve of 'experts'. Most people spend a lot of time trying to make sense of everyday experiences, whether in their personal lives or at work. Managers are in some respects paid to determine actions in uncertain circumstances, to create order out of chaos. In this context research can be seen as a way of accelerating the process of understanding, and hence it should lead not only to a better understanding of management, but also to a better understanding *for* managers about how best to go about their work.

This leads directly to our second point. In the past, much attention has been given to describing, coding and counting events, often at the expense of understanding *why* things are happening. This has led to a predominance of quantitative research methods which are geared, for example, to finding out how many people hold particular views, or variations in measures of corporate performance. By contrast, qualitative methods might concentrate on exploring in much greater depth the nature and origins of people's viewpoints, or the reasons for, and consequences of, the choice of corporate performance criteria. In this book, therefore, we intend to redress this balance a little, by giving more prominence to the use of qualitative methods, without totally abandoning consideration of the design and application of quantitative methods.

Our third point is that it is unwise to conduct research without an awareness of the philosophical and political issues that lie in the background. The decision to study a topic in a particular way always involves some kind of philosophical choice about what is important. A study that examined variations in corporate performance for a range of companies in France during the decade following the 1973 oil crisis would need to assume that the performance of any company was tangible and ultimately reducible to a single number for any period of time. The alternative would be to see the idea of 'performance' as unique to each company and the creation of endless discussion and negotiation between individuals and coalitions who are involved with that company. In the former case it is the numbers, and in the latter case it is the perceptions, that are important; it is for the researcher to decide where the emphasis should lie.

While philosophical issues may seem hidden in research methods, it is hard to escape political and ethical factors in management research. Access to companies can be obstructed by managers if they see a piece of research being harmful to their, or their company's, interests; and there is always the danger of research data and results being used out of context to strengthen the case of one group against another. The researcher should therefore be prepared to confront ethical issues, and to be aware of his or her own values in this process.

These are some of the main assumptions, or prejudices, that have given rise to this book. They influence both the overall structure and our choice of content, particularly in the second and third parts. In this first part we consider a number of preliminary aspects of management research, and this chapter begins by considering the nature of management and the different forms that research may take in this context.

What is management?

There are many views about what constitutes 'management', and clearly the notion of management as an activity is not new: the Egyptians built their pyramids, the Chinese built the Great Wall and the Mesopotamians learned to irrigate their land and wall their cities. All these feats required a high degree of coordination and, although many involved a 'captive labour force', there must have been some organisation of work, even if rudimentary. Formal records of production management techniques can be traced back to Mencius (372–289BC). This Chinese philosopher dealt with models and systems, and pointed to the advantages of the division of labour, which puts the concepts rediscovered 2,000 years later into perspective.

A distinction can be made between management as a 'cadre' of people, and management as an activity. Management as a cadre are those members of an organisation who carry the title of manager and who commonly share similar beliefs about their status and right to manage. Usually the title 'manager' is given to people in the organisation hierarchy who are at one or more levels above 'first-line' supervision. This definition can be applied most easily in a traditional manufacturing company. However, with the growth of the service sector, and the move from hierarchical structures to flatter organisation structures which stress the importance of commitment, multi-skilled teams, minimum status and harmonisation, the traditional means of defining a manager is becoming increasingly problematic. Handy (1989) notes this change, when he says that in the new organisation everyone will need to have the skills of a manager. Organisation members will not only need their own professional or technical expertise but will also rapidly acquire responsibility for money, people and projects.

The modern use of the term 'management' derives from the USA, with the requirement for business and entrepreneurial skills at the turn of the century when American industries and railroads were developing very rapidly (Lawrence, 1986). From these beginnings management was put forward as an important subject that could, and should, be taught in higher education.

The creation of management schools led to greater systematisation of techniques and knowledge. Much of this was based on the principles that managers had distilled from their own experiences. Two of the dominant figures during this period were Taylor (1947) and Fayol (1916), who classified the main functions that managers should perform, such as: planning, organising, coordinating and controlling. Although this *classical* view of management has much face validity, later researchers were to show that these functions had little resemblance to what managers, whether good or bad, actually did in their work (Mintzberg, 1973).

A further impetus was given to management after 1945 by the widespread development of business schools outside the US, and by the attempts of US schools to seek greater academic respectability for their disciplines. In their influential report sponsored by the Ford Foundation, Gordon and Howell (1959) stressed the importance of analytic approaches to management and the need to select students and faculty on their academic credentials rather than their managerial calibre. This led to the strengthening of academic disciplines, such as finance, marketing, operations research and organisational behaviour.

During the 1960s the view developed that the key to effective management was the ability to take decisions, particularly under conditions of uncertainty (Simon, 1959; Cyert and March, 1963). This *decision theory* approach therefore emphasised the importance of techniques that could be used to analyse the environment within which decisions must be made, and ways of reaching decisions which will work as well as possible, even if they are not completely ideal. Quantitative methods of analysis and model-building still dominate the curricula of many business schools, especially in the USA and France.

With both the classical and decision theory approaches there is some confusion between what management *is*, and what it *ought to be*; because of this confusion they are often described as 'normative' theories of management. Each theory also has implications about the questions that are worth researching, and the methods that should be used to do this. However, during the last two decades these theories have come under considerable attack from two separate, but related, quarters.

The classical view has been attacked by researchers such as Stewart (1967), Mintzberg (1973) and Kotter (1982), who, as we have indicated above, found almost no evidence of managers behaving as they are supposed to do. Instead of standing back and directing enterprises strategically, most managers, even top ones, spend most of their time talking to people; they work long hours at an unrelenting pace; their work patterns are varied, fragmented and reactive; and there is rarely any time for planning ahead and anticipating crises. Consequently, they argue, there is little point in trying to get them to behave according to the classical textbooks. Rather, managers should be helped to deal with the realities of their jobs through managing their own time and becoming more skilled at working and negotiating with others.

The second line of attack has come from employers, and has been readily assisted by a number of academics and researchers (Livingston, 1971; Hayes and Abernathy, 1980; Peters and Waterman, 1982). The main argument is that the emphasis on analytic techniques is of limited value, and may even be harmful to companies. It is more important for managers to exhibit leadership, to provide collective visions, and to mould the culture and values of the organisation in appropriate directions.

Even the academic establishment in the USA is beginning to accept that there may be some truth in these points, with the publication of a mildly critical report about how the system should adapt to meet the challenges of the future (Porter and McKibbin, 1988). But there may well be too much inertia in a system that produces around 80,000 MBAs and 250,000 undergraduates per annum: any changes are likely to involve minor adjustments to the curriculum, rather than the wholesale restructuring that would follow from adoption of a distinctly different philosophy of management education.

The four approaches described above are by no means the only views about what management is, or should be; but they have been important historically. The reason for reviewing them briefly here is to demonstrate that there are many views of what constitutes 'management', and to emphasise that whichever view one adopts is likely to influence both the focus and the methods of management research.

Why is management research distinctive?

At the present time the majority of books on research methods derive from disciplines such as sociology, education and psychology. While we still rely very heavily on these ourselves, we feel that management research poses some unusual problems and therefore the general approaches need rethinking. There are three main things that make management distinctive as a focus for research.

Firstly, despite the progress towards creating distinct disciplines within management, the practice of management is largely *eclectic*: managers need to be able to work across technical, cultural and functional boundaries; they need to be able to draw on knowledge developed by other disciplines such as sociology, anthropology, economics, statistics and mathematics. The dilemma for the researcher, then, is whether to examine management from the perspective of one discipline, or whether to adopt a cross-disciplinary approach. It seems that the former is the safer course for those who wish to gain respectability from academic peers; but the latter is more likely to produce results that are of use to practising managers.

Secondly, managers tend to be *powerful* and busy people. They are unlikely to allow research access to their organisations unless they can see some commercial or personal advantage to be derived from it. This means, as we shall see in Chapter 4, that access for fieldwork can be very difficult and may be hedged with many conditions about confidentiality and publication rights; feasible research questions may be determined more by access possibilities than by theoretical considerations. Nowadays, managers have to count very carefully the cost of their time and therefore short interviews are likely to be much more feasible than unstructured observations and discussion.

Thirdly, management requires both thought and *action*. Not only do most managers feel that research should lead to practical consequences, they are also quite capable of taking action themselves in the light of research results. Thus research methods either need to incorporate within them the potential for taking action, or need to take account of the practical consequences that will probably ensue.

Admittedly none of these factors is unique to management research. The problem of multiple disciplines exists in educational research, and the access problem is very evident in organisational sociology. But the possible combination of all three suggests to us that some of the traditional assumptions and practices in social research may well need rethinking. This is what we hope we are beginning to do in this book.

Outcomes and forms of research

However, for the time being we need to start with some of the existing concepts and ideas, and consider how they relate to management research. In this section, therefore, we look at some of the main classifications of research: pure, applied and action research. These are distinguished primarily by the outcomes that are assumed to emerge – although, as ever, the distinctions do not hold clearly in practice.

Pure research
The key feature of 'pure' research is that it is intended to lead to theoretical developments; there may, or may not, be any practical implications. There are at least three forms that theoretical developments may take. Firstly there is the popular view that scientific research is about *discovery*. This is when a totally new idea or explanation emerges from empirical research which may revolutionise thinking on that particular topic. A well known example in management is the Hawthorne Effect, where research into the effect of physical conditions at work led to the discovery that social conditions, including the act of carrying out research, have a major impact on productivity and work behaviour.

Discoveries are rare and unpredictable, and we will discuss the reasons for this further in the next chapter. A more common outcome from research is what we call an *invention*: where a new technique, method or idea is created to deal with a particular kind of problem. Examples would include Scientific Management (Taylor, 1947), or Total Quality Management (Walton, 1989). These are based on direct experiences of their inventors, rather than exhaustive fieldwork; they all have considerable commercial potential, but were produced to deal with a general kind of problem.

We call the third type of outcome from pure research *reflection*. This is where an existing theory, technique or group of ideas is re-examined, possibly in a different organisational or social context. For example, one could examine to what extent Herzberg's theory of motivation (Herzberg et al., 1959), which was developed in the USA, could be applied in UK or German companies. Results from the comparison could lead to revision and modification of the theory or to further ideas about cultural differences. This form of research is less spectacular than discovery or invention, but very widely used, especially for doctoral theses.

One of the key features of pure research is that its results are openly disseminated through books, articles, conference papers or theses, although these are likely to be addressed mainly to an academic audience. Indeed, this is seen as a major responsibility for the researcher.

Applied research
Applied research is intended to lead to the solution of specific problems, and usually involves working with clients who identify the problems and, if you are lucky, pay for their solution. This is quite commonly used at the Masters' level, although to gain academic approval it is still important to try to *explain* what is happening, rather than simply describing things. Phillips and Pugh (1987) use a similar distinction between the 'why' and the 'what' questions in stressing that genuine research must include consideration of 'why' questions. It is important to be critical of ideas and methods used and to consider the quality of evidence introduced in support of an idea. One common form of applied research is the evaluation of the process and results of particular courses of action – such as the reorganisation of a department, the introduction of new technology or the training of new graduates in a company.

The results of applied research always need to be reported to the client, but there should also be potential to discuss their wider implications in journals and other publications aimed at practitioners. However, this may raise issues of confidentiality and control of information, and we discuss these in more detail in Chapter 4.

Action research

A number of research approaches have developed in management which do not fit neatly into either of the above categories, and we have grouped these under the heading of action research. These start from the view that research should lead to change, and therefore that change should be incorporated into the research process itself.

Classical action research starts from the idea that if you want to understand something well you should try changing it, and this is most frequently adopted in Organisation Development (French and Bell, 1978; Holmen, 1979). 'New paradigm' research stresses the importance of establishing collaboration between researcher and researched, leading to the development of shared understandings (Reason and Rowan, 1981). This is most easily done when working with individuals or small groups. Finally, 'Action Learning' is not so much a research approach, as an educational process that makes extensive use of action research methods. Students are expected to learn from tackling real problems in their own, or others', organisations, and these projects are reviewed regularly within a 'set' of 5–8 students, each of whom are tackling their own projects at the same time. Revans (1980) stresses that projects should be open-ended problems, rather than 'puzzles' with identifiable solutions, and for this reason a focus on change is often chosen.

Because of the collaborative features of action research, participants (the researcher and the researched) are likely to learn a lot from the process itself, and their interest may be in what happens next rather than in any formal account of research findings. But it may still be worth writing up action research as a narrative, so that a record is maintained of how understanding changes and develops over time.

Choosing types of research

As we shall see in Chapters 3 and 4 there are many factors, both political and philosophical, which can influence the way research is designed and conducted in practice. But it is also possible to affect the outcomes by a careful choice of initial style and strategy.

When research is being conducted as part of a higher degree it is usually best to adopt a flexible strategy, because within any learning process there will be mistakes and false starts. If a project is to last for 3–4 months then evaluation research is often the easiest option. This involves looking at some system or practice that already exists and making recommendations as to how it might be changed. The greater the attempt to encourage change, the nearer it will come to pure action research. Involvement in change can lead to rich and interesting results, and it may be a valuable experience for people seeking work in consultancy. The drawbacks are firstly that it may be hard to make a clear end-point to the research, and secondly that it is not easy to draw out the full significance of the experience when writing it up.

More is possible with longer project periods, but even with PhDs the time never seems sufficient for what is being attempted. Doctoral work needs to produce theoretical outcomes, and the easiest ways of doing this are either to replicate known studies with one or two of the variables, such as country or industrial sector, being changed, or to look at a practical problem from two different theoretical perspectives. It is through contrasts that new ideas and insights are most easily created. It is quite unrealistic to expect great discoveries from every doctoral project, but it seems that the chances will be improved if one incorporates both pure and applied elements in the research.

One other strategy is to avoid gathering any first-hand data, and to focus on analysis of others' work. This is the realm of 'armchair theorising' or scholarship. It is less valued at the moment in universities which are rated on their ability to attract the funds required for expensive empirical research; but nonetheless it is important because with empirical research the requirements of data collection often overwhelm careful analysis and reflection on what it all means.

In conclusion, although it is possible to give advice about research methods this can rarely be definitive. The researcher must be prepared continually to use her own judgement – and this, as Buchanan (1980) suggests, is one of the most important outcomes from the use of research projects in management development programmes. Research is always hedged about with uncertainty and risk. Those who learn to work effectively and independently with this uncertainty will find they possess a skill that can be transferred very easily into management roles.

Overview of the book

We have divided the book into three main parts. This initial part is intended to introduce the nature of research, and to look at some of the factors, particularly personal and social ones, that can lead to successful research outcomes. In Part Two we examine two key aspects of management research: the philosophical and political

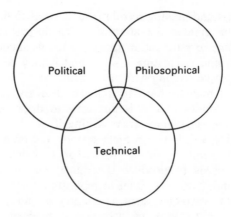

Figure 1.1   *Main aspects of management research*

aspects. The third part concentrates on the technical aspects of gathering data and on the problems of completing research work. As we have implied above, there is an emphasis on the use of qualitative methods in this part, but we also give some consideration to the use of quantitative methods. These main aspects, all of which overlap slightly with each other, are illustrated in Figure 1.1. We also intended, at one stage, to add a fourth circle which would cover practical implications. But it soon became apparent that practical and theoretical issues needed to be dealt with at the same time, and that they could not easily be separated. Thus we have attempted, whenever possible, to give practical implications and examples throughout the book.

Although some sections of Part Three may be treated as a 'cookbook', with readers dipping in and out at their convenience, there is a progressive logic to the other parts of the book. Terms and concepts are defined when they are first introduced, and therefore their usage may be misunderstood if the reader does not start at the beginning and finish at the end. However, this logical progression may not seem appropriate to all readers, and they are welcome to plot whatever path they choose, both through this book and the research labyrinth. They can but find their own way in both cases.

2

The Ingredients of Successful Research

It should be clear by now that there is no simple way of ensuring that research will be successful. The types and contexts of research vary so widely that 'ideal' strategies will also differ from situation to situation. If the research is worth doing then one is likely to be dealing with a problem which is not fully understood, and for which the ideal course of investigation cannot be charted in advance with any certainty. Nevertheless there are a number of factors that seem to increase the chances of research being successful – all things being equal. We discuss four such factors in this chapter: motivation, support, style and personal qualities. The prospective researcher should be aware of her own strengths and weaknesses before starting out, and we show how to appraise them. The chapter concludes with some thoughts about one of the biggest problems of all: getting started.

Motivation

Phillips and Pugh (1987) offer some pertinent advice on how to get a PhD. The first of their seven points is 'not to *want* a PhD' (p. 29), the point being that much determination and single-mindedness is required with any form of research. From the outset people need to be very committed to conducting and completing the work because the task invariably becomes greater than it appeared to be at first. Here we distinguish between three apparent motives for researchers: research as a vehicle for learning within management courses; research as a basis for personal growth; and research as a means of dealing with real problems at work.

It is now very common for management courses, particularly if they lead to postgraduate qualifications, to contain an element of research. Many taught courses use the project or dissertation as a kind of 'capstone', as a way of integrating the different elements, and of giving the student some experience of the outside world. Some students treat the project instrumentally, as a way of achieving a pass on the course; some may use it to obtain contacts and credibility which will help with job-hunting. Others find themselves getting absorbed by the project, and excited at the novel possibility of studying something in depth.

This links to the second main source of motivation, *personal growth*. There are many possibilities here. People may register for research degrees because they want to be given an external discipline for examining something in which they have long held a passionate interest; they may want to prove to themselves that they can do research; or they may simply want to belong to a research 'community' for a few years. People who are nearing retirement often come into this category; so, too, do people who have had earlier failures in the educational system.

The third source comes from a recognition that research experiences may contribute directly to enhancing *managerial skills*. As we suggested in the first chapter, research may help to develop judgement; this includes the skills of judging what information is important, how and when to obtain it, and how best to communicate results. It is also likely to strengthen independence, because of the lack of prior rules and the need to initiate, structure and monitor progress on one's own for most of the time. Both of these skills are likely to become more important for managers as the business environment becomes more complex and unpredictable.

Some people may well have all three of the above reasons for doing research. At the very least it helps to have a combination of 'internal' and 'external' pressures, such as a strong interest in a particular topic and clear expectations and deadlines from a sponsor, or your family. At the outset it is worth considering your motives carefully. If you have sufficient driving forces, continue; if not, research may not be for you.

Support

Research work can be very demanding on the individual. Many uncertainties, doubts and crises enter into most research projects. From her interviews with students, Phillips (1984) has identified seven main stages in the process of conducting a PhD. These are: enthusiasm, isolation, increasing interest, increasing independence, boredom, frustration and a job to be finished. Not every research project will necessarily go through precisely the same seven stages, but ups and downs are inevitable. The emotional cost of these crises can be quite high, and hence it is important to consider the support, both technical and emotional, that is available.

When the research is part of an academic degree the most obvious source of support is the supervisor or tutor. But not all supervisors are ideal. The following points are based on a combination of our and others' experiences of the behaviour of supervisors who seem most successful at this task. These may be taken into account by those who are able to influence their choice of supervision. Firstly, the supervisor must possess some technical expertise, although a general knowledge of the research area and of relevant methodologies is perhaps more useful than a very deep knowledge of the subject to be investigated. Phillips (1984) found that the better supervisors tended to set regular, and realistic, deadlines, but that they did not interfere too much with the detail of the work. A 'responsive' style seems most appropriate if the researcher is to be encouraged to become autonomous and independent; and, we would add, the supervisor must be prepared and able to respond quite rapidly to any problems or written work. He or she should be prepared to 'turn round' draft chapters and reviews within days or, at the most, a week or two. Availability is very important, and for this reason the 'guru' with a string of brilliant publications, but who is always out of the country may not necessarily be the best supervisor.

The relationship between supervisor and student is also important because it must be strong enough to cope with the different stages of the research process. Ideally there should be mutual commitment between the two parties, and this should, if possible, result from the initial choice and negotiation process. It should also be recognised that the role of the supervisor can be difficult at times. From our own experiences as supervisors there is often a nagging doubt that the advice one is giving may be wrong. There is also the continuing dilemma between providing feedback which highlights weakness in a piece of work, and providing praise and encouragement to try harder. The way out of this dilemma is to put across the message: 'This is fine in the following respects . . . but it could be made even better in these areas . . . and the way I'd go about it is . . . .'

Not everyone is lucky enough to have a supervisor, and even for those who do there may be elements of ambiguity in the relationship. Hence it is always worth considering alternative sources of support. One of the best forms of support can come from colleagues, either through naturally occurring friendships, or through a 'support set' – a group of 4 or 5 researchers committed to meeting regularly every few weeks to discuss their research progress and problems. It helps if the members of this set are working in related fields, but they should not be too close because this can sometimes generate conflict and competition. This 'set' may have a tutor (or set advisor) who can help it to organise itself, and possibly provide specialist advice and support. The members of the set should be able to use it to 'bounce' ideas off each other and, particularly for those who are researching part-time, to provide contact with others who may be going through the same experiences of doubt, confusion and disillusionment as themselves.

In Chapter 4 we discuss a little further the problem of support, and the potential of devices such as 'sets'. However, at this stage we would emphasise the need to consider at the outset what forms of support you have, whether professional or domestic. The most common cause of 'failure' in research is simply 'giving up'!

Style and creativity

In the previous section we explained why emotional support was a key factor in the successful completion of research work. Here we focus more on ways of ensuring that the research will be of good quality and will contain some originality. We argue that this is determined largely by the personal style and approach adopted by the researcher.

A fascinating study into the personal factors that contribute to discoveries in medicine is provided by Austin (1978), an American neuro-surgeon who had become dissatisfied by the trite explanations provided by scientists about how great discoveries come about. He differentiated four factors, or forms of 'chance', which seem to underlie many of these discoveries.

1 Chance 1 is simply *blind luck*. Although this may often be important, it is unlikely to be the only reason for a breakthrough. Relying on blind luck can take a long time. Austin reminds us that if you wait for 13 spades to turn up in a hand of cards at bridge, the odds are 635 million to one against.
2 Chance 2 derives from the researcher being *in motion*. Nobody, it has been said, trips over anything whilst sitting down. The greater the curiosity, resilience and persistence of the researcher, the more likely he is to find something of significance.
3 Chance 3 comes from having a *prepared mind* and being ready to see new relationships and solutions. This means being aware of past research that has been conducted, through searching the literature and talking to other researchers, whilst at the same time being prepared to think outside existing frameworks and knowledge.
4 Chance 4 is a product of *individualised action*. This means encouraging distinctive, even eccentric, hobbies and lifestyles. In particular, the researcher should try to take a broad interest in people and other disciplines. Creativity is often born from associations and links made across traditional boundaries.

There are many examples of scientific research where the above elements of 'chance' are demonstrated. But the illustration that Austin himself uses is Fleming's discovery of penicillin in 1928.

In an interview twenty years later, Fleming commented that the discovery of penicillin was almost entirely a matter of luck: 'like winning the Irish Sweepstake'. But Austin shows that it was not only a matter of blind luck. Fleming, by all accounts, was a tireless researcher, his great aim being to discover a new antiseptic, and even after the penicillin discovery he was extremely busy making and selling antibacterial vaccines. Thus he was a man who was constantly in motion.

Chance 3, the prepared mind, relates to the mental processes of seeing the effect on colonies of bacteria when a stray spore of a rare mould fell by accident onto his culture dish. Fleming's mind was, in fact, very well prepared. Nine years earlier he had discovered the bacterial enzyme lysozyme when . . . 'whilst suffering from a cold, his own nasal drippings had found their way into a culture dish. He noted that the bacteria round the mucus were killed and astutely followed up the lead' (Austin, 1978: 74). The parallels between these and other experiences would be easy to perceive. Chance 4, individualised action, comes into the story because Fleming was a keen swimmer and water polo player. He had not chosen to train and work at the old St Mary's hospital because of the excellence of its scientific facilities, but because it had a good swimming pool. The laboratories were basic, badly equipped, cold and 'contaminated by organisms swirling in and out of the London fog' (Austin, 1978: 92). This made them a particularly good breeding ground for bacteria and stray spores!

In this example it is possible to see all four forms of chance at work, and Austin suggested that major discoveries are most likely to take place when several forms coincide. This is what he calls the unifying observation of the Fleming effect.

Unfortunately not all researchers are destined to make major discoveries. Indeed it is wise to content oneself with what we have termed invention or reflection; discovery is but a bonus, which may be made more likely by following Austin's prescriptions. The bulk of research is much more humble.

Phillips and Pugh (1987) identify three characteristics of good research, whether it be grand or humble, which distinguish it from activities such as decision-making or consultancy. Firstly it is based on an *open system of thought*. This requires continual testing, review and criticism of others' ideas, and a willingness to hazard new ideas, even without half a dozen references to support them. Secondly, one must always be prepared to *examine data critically*, and to request the evidence behind conclusions drawn by others.

Thirdly, one should always try to *generalise the research*, but within stated limits. This means attempting to extract understanding from one situation and to apply it to as many other situations as possible.

While few researchers would disagree with the first two characteristics, there are those who feel that the third denies the uniqueness of each individual or organisation. However, it seems that all three, plus the points made by Austin (1978), should be considered carefully by those wishing to improve the quality of their research.

Personal qualities

The qualities required by researchers are not easy to define. Turner (1988) compares the researcher to an expert cook, who finds it difficult to explain what he does but claims that the end result is evidence of his proficiency. In order to develop these qualities to the full, a further analogy is suggested – that of apprenticeship. The implication is that although the necessary skills can be explained, they cannot be fully acquired without experience.

Knowing yourself

In this section we have listed what we believe to be the important qualities of researchers. These are based partly on our own experiences and on some of the sources described above. The resulting qualities we have classified according to whether they comprise knowledge, skills or personal attributes. This classification is based substantially on Burgoyne and Stuart's (1976) work into the attributes of effective managers, and it is here that we think the greatest transferability lies between managing and researching. The skills and knowledge areas are progressively more specific to the conduct of research. These are 'core' qualities, which are important in any form of research, and are listed in Figure 2.1. Those interested in a rough diagnosis of their strengths and weaknesses as researchers can rate themselves on each quality using the following scale:

4 Possess to a high degree
3 Possess to a moderate degree
2 Possess to a limited extent
1 Have virtually none of these

Any ratings below 3 may be cause for concern (with the possible exception of item 5). What to do about any apparent deficiencies

Core qualities: checklist

Knowledge	*Skills*	*Personal qualities*
1 Awareness of different assumptions about the world ☐	7 Ability to plan, organise and manage one's time ☐	13 Awareness of own strengths, weaknesses and values ☐
2 Awareness of methods of data collection ☐	8 Ability to search libraries and other sources ☐	14 Clarity of thought ☐
3 Awareness of different research designs ☐	9 Ability to gain support and cooperation from others ☐	15 Sensitivity to events and feelings ☐
4 Knowledge of immediate subject of study ☐	10 Ability to structure and argue a case in writing ☐	16 Emotional resilience ☐
5 Knowledge of related subjects/disciplines ☐	11 Ability to defend and argue views orally ☐	17 Flexibility ☐
6 Knowledge of key networks and contacts in one's chosen research area ☐	12 Ability to learn from experience ☐	18 Creativity ☐
Total ☐	*Total* ☐	*Total* ☐

Figure 2.1 *Qualities of competent researchers*

is, of course, a different matter. As a generalisation: 'knowledge' can be acquired by reading and talking, or by attending courses; 'skills' can be acquired through practising them, in either a simulated or a real environment; and 'personal qualities' can be acquired, with much difficulty, through life or educational experiences. This book certainly cannot offer everything. It provides a reasonable coverage of items 1, 2, 3, 8 and 10; and it touches on 6, 7, 9, 12 and 13. As for the rest, they may be acquired most easily by working with other researchers, in the form of apprenticeship suggested by Turner (1988).

We believe that the qualities in Figure 2.1 should be possessed by any researcher working in the management area – which is why we have called them 'core' qualities. Beyond a certain point, however, specialisation begins to creep in. One form of specialisation depends upon whether the researcher is following a primarily quantitative or qualitative path. We have commented briefly on this issue in Chapter 1 and will return to it in more detail in later chapters. Depending on the position taken, researchers will need to be skilled in the use of different methods for such things as seeking information, analysing data and presenting research results. Those following the quantitative path will need to be competent in areas such as survey design, sampling methods and statistical analysis; those following the qualitative path may need skills in conducting 'in-depth' interviews, making field notes, coding and interpreting transcripts, and so on. In Part Three we give extensive guidance on the choice and application of qualitative methods, followed by a more limited review of possible quantitative methods.

Getting started

It is very rare for students to have a clear focus at the outset of their research, and yet many find the lack of a clear focus is a major impediment to getting started. It often takes a whole year to find an acceptable focus, which may include false starts, drifting and moments of despondency and elation. Indeed, the whole research project may be seen as a continuous process of focusing.

Those who are working on shorter, more applied, projects may be more fortunate in having a problem or question given to them by their supervisors, tutors or clients (we discuss the different influences on the research 'question' in Chapter 4). The situation for people working in the natural sciences is similar, because work and funding is often parcelled up into groups of related projects, which are largely predetermined.

Whatever the situation, it is worth getting started as quickly as possible. This means defining a provisional area of interest, reviewing relevant literature (see the Appendix for guidelines), and gathering some data relevant to the focus. One way of thinking about a topic is to produce a scheme or model of the issues involved. An example of such a scheme developed for some French marketing research is shown in Figure 2.2. In a Masters' project this may be all one can do anyway. In a doctoral project it might form the pilot investigation of a larger study, or it might have to be completely jettisoned at a later stage. In this case there are most likely to be indirect benefits in terms of the contacts, ideas or techniques one encounters on the way. At the very least, this is invoking Austin's (1978) second principle of being 'in motion'.

Once possible topics have been identified it might be worth considering them in the light of a small study conducted by our colleague Andrzej Huczyski, who looked at why certain management ideas and theories come to the fore and gain popularity at the expense of equally well researched and valid alternatives. He found that the successful theories have three features in common:

1 The general topic or area has appeared repeatedly in the

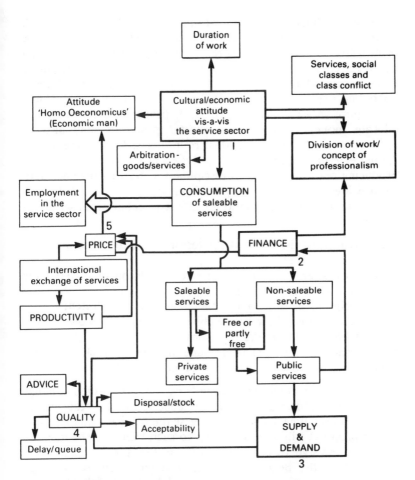

Figure 2.2 *Scheme: Determinants of growth in employment in the service sector. From:* Promouvoir la qualité dans les services pour développer l'emploi [Promotion of quality in the service sector as an aid to growth in employment] *(Usunier, 1986)*

literature over a long period of time (for example, leadership, strategy, decision-making).

2 The idea reaches its audience at a time when it becomes acceptable (such as the studies around 1980 of why Japan was overtaking the USA).

3 The individual researcher has the ability and opportunity to promote and capitalise on the idea (for example, Tom Peters is an outstanding self-publicist).

Sooner or later it is worth writing a research proposal which summarises what the project is about, and how it is to be investigated. Some institutions require a proposal from all prospective research candidates before registration, while others require a formal proposal after 12–15 months if a decision is required about upgrading registration from MPhil to PhD levels. Research Councils require very detailed (but concise!) proposals before they will allocate money to applicants; shorter proposals may also be required at the beginning of Masters' projects. Even if there is no formal external requirement to produce a proposal, the exercise of producing one is a very good discipline for drawing together half-formed ideas in the early stages of research.

The main items that should go into a research proposal are as follows:

1 a statement of the focus of the research and the main questions to be investigated;
2 an explanation of how it relates to, builds on or differs from previous work in the field;
3 a description of how, and what, data will be collected;
4 an explanation of how data will be interpreted and how this will relate back to the initial questions posed;
5 comments on the practical value of the research, and any problems that may be encountered in its conduct.

The document should not normally exceed 3,000 words although the amount of detail required will depend on the scale of the project and the time available. Likewise the emphasis and structure of the proposal will vary according to such things as the intended audience, the style of research and the methods to be used. As we suggested at the beginning of this chapter, there is no single formula for ensuring that research will be successful. One must always exercise judgement according to the particular circumstances that prevail. The next part of this book is intended to explain many of the factors that are contingent upon research, and thus to assist the researcher in making informed choices as he or she progresses.

3

The Philosophy of Research Design

'It is a capital mistake to theorise before one has data'.

Conan Doyle

The relationship between data and theory is an issue that has been hotly debated by philosophers for many centuries. Failure to think through philosophical issues such as this, while not necessarily fatal, can seriously affect the quality of management research. That is why we have decided to begin the central part of the book with a discussion of the main philosophical choices underlying management research.

To be more specific, there are at least three reasons why an understanding of philosophical issues is very useful. Firstly, it can help to clarify research designs, and by 'research design' we mean more than simply the methods by which data is collected and analysed. It is the overall configuration of a piece of research: what kind of evidence is gathered from where, and how such evidence is interpreted in order to provide good answers to the basic research question. Secondly, a knowledge of philosophy can help the researcher to recognise which designs will work and which will not. It should enable the researcher to avoid going up too many blind alleys and indicate the limitations of particular approaches. Thirdly, a knowledge of philosophy can help the researcher identify, and even create, designs that may be outside his or her past experience. It may also help the researcher to adapt research designs according to the constraints of different subject or knowledge structures.

Arguments, criticisms and debates are central to the progress of philosophy. But within the social sciences it seems that such debates take the form either of denigrating the other point of view, or of completely ignoring its existence. We shall try to provide here a balanced view of the philosophical positions underlying different research methods, and to do this we have had to return to some of the original sources of these positions. The chapter therefore starts by reviewing a central debate amongst social science philosophers. We then go on to look at the implications of this debate for a number of fundamental choices in research design, and we conclude the chapter with a look at the way different research contexts and disciplinary structures may affect research methods.

Two main traditions

The philosophies

There is a long-standing debate in the social sciences about the most appropriate philosophical position from which methods should be derived. In the red corner is phenomenology; in the blue corner is positivism. Each of these positions has to some extent been elevated into a stereotype, often by the opposing side. Although it is now possible to draw up comprehensive lists of assumptions and methodological implications associated with each position, it is not possible to identify any one philosopher who ascribes to all aspects of one particular view. Indeed, occasionally an author from one corner produces ideas which belong more neatly to those of the other corner.

Also, when one looks at the practice of research, as we shall see below, even self-confessed extremists do not hold consistently to one position or the other. Although there has been a trend away from positivism towards phenomenology over the last few years, there are many researchers, especially in the management field, who adopt a pragmatic view by deliberately combining methods drawn from both traditions.

So what are these traditions? Let us start with *positivism*. The key idea of positivism is that the social world exists externally, and that its properties should be measured through objective methods, rather than being inferred subjectively through sensation, reflection or intuition. The French philosopher, Auguste Comte (1853), was an early and influential proponent of this view, as he said: 'All good intellects have repeated, since Bacon's time, that there can be no real knowledge but that which is based on observed facts.'

This statement contains two assumptions: firstly, that reality is external and objective; secondly, that knowledge is only of significance if it is based on observations of this external reality. There follow from this a number of implications, although not all of them were proposed by Comte:

1 *independence*: the observer is independent of what is being observed;
2 *value-freedom*: the choice of what to study, and how to study it, can be determined by objective criteria rather than by human beliefs and interests;
3 *causality*: the aim of social sciences should be to identify causal explanations and fundamental laws that explain regularities in human social behaviour;
4 *hypothetico-deductive*: science proceeds through a process of hypothesising fundamental laws and then deducing what kinds of observations will demonstrate the truth or falsity of these hypotheses;
5 *operationalisation*: concepts need to be operationalised in a way which enables facts to be measured quantitatively;
6 *reductionism*: problems as a whole are better understood if they are reduced into the simplest possible elements;
7 *generalisation*: in order to be able to generalise about regularities in human and social behaviour it is necessary to select samples of sufficient size;
8 *cross-sectional analysis*: such regularities can most easily be identified by making comparisons of variations across samples.

It is worth repeating that these propositions are not simply the view of any single philosopher; they are a collection of points that have come to be associated with the positivist viewpoint. Some 'positivists' would disagree with some of these statements. Comte, for example, did not agree with the principle of reductionism. Wittgenstein argued strongly in his early work that all factual propositions can be reduced into elementary propositions which are completely independent of one another. But in his later work he challenged his earlier view on the grounds that elementary propositions such as colours could still be logically related to each other (Pears, 1971). So philosophers within the same school not only disagree with each other; they may also change their own views significantly over time.

The view that positivism provides the best way of investigating human and social behaviour originated as a reaction to metaphysical speculation (Aiken, 1956). This philosophy has developed into a distinctive paradigm over the last one and a half centuries. The term 'paradigm' has come into vogue among social scientists recently, particularly through the work of Thomas Kuhn. Kuhn (1962) used it to describe the progress of scientific discoveries in practice, rather than how they are subsequently reconstructed within textbooks and academic journals. Most of the time, according to Kuhn, science progresses in tiny steps, which refine and extend what is already 'known'. But occasionally experiments start to produce results that do not fit into existing theories and patterns. Then, perhaps many years later, a Galileo or Einstein proposes a new way of looking at things which can account for both the old and the new observations.

It is evident from these examples, and from the discovery of penicillin by Fleming, as described in Chapter 2, that major scientific advances are not produced by a logical and rational application of scientific method. They result from independent and creative thinking which goes outside the boundaries of existing ideas. The result of this is a 'scientific revolution' which not only provides new theories, but which may also alter radically the way people see the world, and the kind of questions that scientists consider important to investigate. This combination of new theories and questions is referred to as a new paradigm.

The new paradigm that has arisen during the last half century, largely in reaction to the application of positivism to the social sciences, stems from the view that the world and 'reality' are not objective and exterior, but that they are socially constructed and given meaning by people (Husserl, 1946). As one might expect, this 'phenomenology' is not logically derived from positivism in any way.

Inevitably many different variants are associated more or less closely with phenomenology. These include interpretive sociology (Habermas, 1970), naturalistic inquiry (Lincoln and Guba, 1986), social constructionism (Berger and Luckman, 1966), qualitative methodology (Taylor and Bodgan, 1984) and 'new paradigm' inquiry (Reason and Rowan, 1981). Each of these takes a slightly different stance in the application of phenomenology and in the features of positivism that it finds most distasteful.

The starting point, as we have said, is the idea that reality is socially constructed rather than objectively determined. Hence the task of the social scientist should not be to gather facts and measure how often certain patterns occur, but to appreciate the different constructions and meanings that people place upon their experience. One should therefore try to understand and explain why people have different experiences, rather than search for external causes and fundamental laws to explain their behaviour. Human action arises from the sense that people make of different situations, rather than as a direct response from external stimuli.

The implications of holding these different views may be seen, for example, in the way researchers might study managerial stress. The social constructionist would be interested in the aspects of

Subjectivist	Objectivist

• Projection of human imagination

    • Social construction

        • Symbolic discourse

            • Contextual field of information

                • Concrete process

                    • Concrete structure

Figure 3.1 *Different assumptions about the nature of reality (after Morgan and Smircich, 1980)*

work that managers consider to be 'stressful', and perhaps in the strategies that they develop for managing these aspects. She would therefore arrange to talk with a few managers about their jobs, about the aspects they find more, or less, difficult, and so on. The positivist, on the other hand, would start with the assumption that occupational stress exists and might then try to measure the levels of stress experienced by managers and how these relate to a number of external stressors such as organisational changes, interpersonal conflicts, negative appraisals, and so on. Measures of stress could be based on standardised verbal reports from the managers, or on physiological factors such as blood pressure or glandular secretions.

There are other philosophical positions that can be taken, however. For example, Morgan and Smircich (1980) identify six distinct ontological assumptions or views about the nature of reality. These form a continuum from extreme subjective to extreme objective approaches as shown in Figure 3.1.

Within the phenomenological or social constructionist viewpoint there are several direct attacks on the assumptions of positivism. One is the notion of 'scientism' (Keat, 1981), which holds that the only knowledge of any significance is that which is derived from the use of objective measures. Another is the view that science itself should be based only on data that can be observed and measured directly. But one of the strongest attacks on positivism has been on its assumptions of value-freedom. This is argued most strongly by Habermas (1970), who points out that any form of knowledge is an instrument of self-preservation. Human interests not only guide the way we think, and the structures of work and

142,947

authority, but they also condition the way we enquire into, and construct our knowledge of, the world. One of the big problems with positivist methods is that they are claimed to be independent of values and interests, yet by and large they support, in practice, the interests of the more powerful members of society. Habermas thus attempts to demonstrate the true relationship between knowledge and interest which is otherwise concealed by the objectivist views of positivism.

As we have mentioned above, the term 'paradigm' has become popularised over recent years, and it therefore tends to be used in many different ways. Henry Mintzberg published a stinging attack on the term as a convenient buzz word for social scientists. It is 'too vague to be pinned down, so it pops up everywhere' (Mintzberg, 1978: 635). In response, Gareth Morgan, who was just about to publish a book about paradigms (Burrell and Morgan, 1979), wrote in its defence. He criticised Mintzberg's 'head-in-the-sand' attitude to a term such as paradigm simply because it is hard to pin down, and proposed instead a way of tidying up its usage. He distinguished between three levels of use: the philosophical level, which reflects basic beliefs about the world; the social level, which provides guidelines about how the researcher should conduct his or her endeavour; and the technical level, which involves specifying the methods and techniques which should ideally be adopted in conducting research (Morgan, 1979).

It is this basic classification that we have used in Figure 3.2, where we attempt to summarise the main differences between the positivist and the phenomenological viewpoints.

These two positions are, of course, the 'pure' versions of each paradigm. Although the basic beliefs may be quite incompatible, when one comes down to the actual research methods and techniques used by researchers the differences are by no means so clear cut and distinct. Increasingly, there is a move amongst management researchers to develop methods and approaches which provide a middle ground, and some bridging between the two extreme viewpoints. These we shall come back to later, but in the meantime we shall look at some classic examples of management and organisational research which are widely acknowledged as representing one or other of these points of view. As we shall see, neither of these are completely pure applications of their respective paradigms.

Examples of practice
First we shall summarise the main features of two major pieces of research that have been conducted largely from the positivist

	Positivist paradigm	Phenomenological paradigm
Basic beliefs:	The world is external and objective	The world is socially constructed and subjective
	Observer is independent	Observer is part of what observed
	Science is value-free	Science is driven by human interests
Researcher should:	focus on facts	focus on meanings
	look for causality and fundamental laws	try to understand what is happening
	reduce phenomena to simplest elements	look at the totality of each situation
	formulate hypotheses and then test them	develop ideas through induction from data
Preferred methods include:	operationalising concepts so that they can be measured	using multiple methods to establish different views of phenomena
	taking large samples	small samples investigated in depth or over time

Figure 3.2 *Key features of positivist and phenomenological paradigms*

paradigm. These are the studies of Pugh and his colleagues at Aston into organisational structure, and the work of Geert Hofstede (1984) on culture.

From 1961 onwards, Pugh and his colleagues conducted a number of large-scale studies of organisations in the West Midlands of England, and in other parts of the world. Their initial, and classic, study involved a sample of 46 organisations with manufacturing or service operations in Greater Birmingham, each one employing at least 250 people. Organisations were selected to provide a good range of sizes and product types. The researchers used a highly structured interview schedule in order to gather data on a total of 132 measures which characterised the structure and context of each organisation. From an analysis of the data across their sample they were able to come up with a number of general conclusions, for example, that size is the most important determinant of organisational structure, and that organisations which are closely dependent on other organisations tend to centralise as many decisions as possible.

These studies achieved international fame when the results were written up in a series of articles that appeared in *Administrative Science Quarterly*, and which were subsequently collected together in a book (Pugh and Hickson, 1976). Possibly their main significance is the way they highlight the authority structures within organisations as key factors to consider when attempting to change, or understand, organisational behaviour. Pugh (1988) feels that this provides a useful counterbalance to the prevailing emphasis on individual and group-related factors.

In a separate account of the ideas and methods behind this work, Pugh (1983) describes himself as an 'unreconstructed positivist'. The key principles that he applies to his work include: focusing on hard data rather than opinions; looking for regularities in the data obtained; and attempting to produce propositions that can generalise from the specific example to the wider population of organisations. He states his view that facts and values can be clearly separated, a view that would of course be hotly disputed by Habermas; but he also adopts a 'systems' view which attempts to examine the full complexity of the data, rather than simply reducing it to its simplest elements. This latter point is perhaps a modification of the positivist view which has arisen partly as a result of developments in the biological sciences (Von Bertalanffy, 1962), and partly as a result of the ability of modern computers to conduct very sophisticated multi-variate analysis of data, provided it is expressed in quantitative terms. Thus, Pugh, by his own admission, sticks fairly closely to the positivist paradigm described above, although in his own research programme he also found it necessary to conduct more detailed case studies of individual organisations in the later stages of his research in order to give a fuller understanding of what was taking place inside (Pugh, 1988).

The second example of positivist research is the classic study of Hofstede (1980) into the effect of national cultures on social and work behaviour. This was based on 116,000 questionnaires completed between 1967 and 1972 by employees of a large American multi-national. Hofstede's data was totally quantitative and its analysis was conducted purely by computer. This analysis indicated four dimensions of national culture:

1 *individualism*: whether a society emphasises individual autonomy as opposed to responsibility to the group;
2 *masculinity*: how far roles in society are differentiated between men and women;
3 *power distance*: the extent to which inequality is accepted by the less powerful people in society;

4 *uncertainty avoidance*: the level of concern about law and order in a society.

Each of these dimensions was statistically independent in the sense that a high score on one would imply neither a high nor a low score on any of the other dimensions. Hofstede, as the researcher, was also distanced and independent from the respondents of the questionnaires. Thus far, Hofstede's highly quantitative research appears to conform closely to the positivist paradigm.

Beyond that, based on his account of the research process (Hofstede, 1980), much of his work simply does not fit the positivist paradigm. For example, he accepts that he is dealing with mental constructs rather than hard objective facts. The four main dimensions of national culture were not formulated as initial hypotheses but only after considerable *post hoc* analysis of the data, and through much reading and discussion with other academic colleagues. Thirdly, he is fully aware of the importance of avoiding assumptions about culture which imply that any one culture is superior to another; and therefore he accepts that his results are not necessarily value-free. Fourthly, he recognises that different methods will provide different perspectives on what is being studied, and therefore it is worth 'triangulating' where possible by using a combination of both quantitative and qualitative methods. Thus, in practice, Hofstede's work contains elements of both paradigms. A dendrogram showing the similarities and differences in the cross-cultural values of the 53 countries included in Hofstede's research is shown in Figure 5.3, in Chapter 5.

On the side of phenomenology or social constructionism is the work of Melville Dalton (1959), who carried out one of the pioneering studies of what managers do in practice. In a later paper (Dalton, 1964) he describes the ideas and philosophies that guided his work, plus some of the ethical dilemmas that were encountered. For a start Dalton rejects the classical 'scientific method' as inappropriate to his work (this is the sequence of hypothesis, observation, testing, and confirmation or disconfirmation of hypothesis). He points out that not only is this method rather idealistic in the sense that natural scientists do not usually follow it themselves (except in the school laboratory), but it was also not feasible to use it in the situation he had chosen. He is opposed to the tendency to quantify and to reduce variables to their smallest components, on the grounds that this loses most of the real meaning of the situation.

Dalton studied the behaviour of managers while working himself within an organisation as a manager. Curiously enough, although he is quite open about his methods and some of the dilemmas this caused, he does not actually say what his role was in the group, but it allowed him 'much unquestioned movement about the firm'. While working in the company he gathered data from his own observations and from those of a number of informants. The informants were clearly aware to some extent of Dalton's purposes, but the rest of the people in the company were largely ignorant of what he was doing – his role was therefore partly overt and partly covert. This clearly meant that he was not in a position to establish any formal experiments to test his ideas, although curiously enough he comments that some of his informants who were aware of his general purpose occasionally deliberately set up situations for him to observe. Thus in no way was Dalton an independent observer of what was taking place; his presence certainly had some impact on the company, even though the nature of that impact is one of the things about which Dalton does not speculate greatly.

Although much of his data was qualitative, in the form of observations by him and comments from his informants, he was not averse to collecting a certain amount of quantitative data such as details of the salaries of managers in the company. This he obtained informally from a secretary in the personnel department in exchange for counselling about whether or not she should marry her boyfriend (in the end she married him, despite Dalton's counselling!)

It is quite clear that Dalton did not start the research with any clearly preconceived set of hypotheses and theories to test; his research grew out of his own 'confusions and irritations'. Rather than trying to formulate explicit hypotheses and guides for his work, he contented himself with framing simple questions about things that were taking place which he did not clearly understand. After looking at a number of specific topics such as the reasons for conflict between different groups of people or the way people accounted for the success of some managers, he finally settled on the overall scheme of attempting to understand the distinction and relationships between official and unofficial action within the organisation.

Dalton was also aware that looking at only one organisation in depth could limit the generalisability of his conclusions. So he supplemented his work with studies through other contacts of several other organisations in the same area. That at least gave him the confidence that the things he had observed in his own company, Milo, were quite likely to be taking place in most other organisations, at least in that part of the United States. As Lawrence (1988) shows, the assumption that there is both a formal and an informal organisation in any institution does not necessarily hold outside the North American culture.

The above studies are often cited as relatively pure examples of either positivist or phenomenological approaches. But, as we have shown, in practice the researchers involved do not hold scrupulously to one or the other approach. Although the distinction between the two paradigms may be very clear at the philosophical level, as Burrell and Morgan (1979) argue, when it comes to the use of quantitative or qualitative methods and to the issues of research design the distinction breaks down (Bulmer, 1988; Punch, 1986). Increasingly, authors and researchers who work in organisations and with managers argue that one should attempt to mix methods to some extent, because it provides more perspectives on the phenomena being investigated. Fielding and Fielding (1986) advocate the use of both quantitative and qualitative methods, and provide examples of how they have been able to combine these different forms of data to good effect in researching organisations such as the National Front in Britain.

The examples they give, however, show how to combine the two kinds of data where the overall direction and significance of the two sources are fairly similar. A problem they do not confront is what to do when quantitative and qualitative forms of data about the same phenomena are in direct opposition. This problem was encountered by Mark and a colleague, Morgan Tanton, in a comparative evaluation study of two executive management programmes, each conducted in a different institution. Qualitative data from interviews and observations showed quite clearly that Course A was superior to Course B, but the quantitative data in the form of student ratings about the two courses showed to a high level of significance that Course B was preferred to Course A. Was this discrepancy caused by the methods used, or could it highlight some unusual features of the two courses being examined? It seemed that the best way to tackle the dilemma was to show the discrepancy to some later course participants and ask whether they had any explanations.

Two reasons emerged as most probable. Firstly, participants commented that they tended to be rather cautious when filling in multiple choice rating forms, because they could never be sure what the data would be used for; therefore, they usually avoided extreme responses in either direction. Secondly, it seemed that the course designs and institutional settings affected the criteria that participants used for evaluating the two courses.

In Institution A the emphasis was on the longer term application of what had been learnt; in Institution B the emphasis was on the immediate quality of sessions conducted within the classroom. Thus it was not surprising that the rating forms which were completed at the end of the course showed one pattern, whereas follow-up interviews conducted some months later showed another.

There are two morals from this story: firstly to be wary of glibly mixing methods simply for the sake of getting a slightly richer picture; and secondly to remember that the reality of what is being investigated may be considerably more complex than the data collection methods are capable of demonstrating.

Before we leave the discussion of how these two paradigms may underlie practical examples, it is worth summarising from a pragmatic view what are seen as some of the strengths and weaknesses of each side. This should help the researcher to choose which methods and aspects are most likely to be of help in a given situation. In the case of quantitative methods and the positivist paradigm, the main strengths are that: they can provide wide coverage of the range of situations; they can be fast and economical; and, particularly when statistics are aggregated from large samples, they may be of considerable relevance to policy decisions. On the debit side, these methods tend to be rather inflexible and artificial; they are not very effective in understanding processes or the significance that people attach to actions; they are not very helpful in generating theories; and because they focus on what is, or what has been recently, they make it hard for the policy-maker to infer what changes and actions should take place in the *future*. As Legge (1984) points out, they may only provide illusions of the 'true' impact of social policies. Most of the data gathered will not be relevant to real decisions although it may be used to support the covert goals of decision-makers.

The strengths and weaknesses of the phenomenological paradigm and associated qualitative methods are fairly complementary. Thus they have strengths in their ability to look at change processes over time, to understand people's meanings, to adjust to new issues and ideas as they emerge, and to contribute to the evolution of new theories. They also provide a way of gathering data which is seen as natural rather than artificial. There are, of course, weaknesses. Data collection can take up a great deal of time and resources, and the analysis and interpretation of data may be very difficult. Qualitative studies often feel very untidy because it is harder to control their pace, progress and end-points. There is also the problem that many people, especially policy-makers, may give low credibility to studies based on a phenomenological approach.

Research design: some choices and issues

As suggested at the start of this chapter, research designs are about organising research activity, including the collection of data, in ways that are most likely to achieve the research aims. There are many potential choices to make when developing a research design, and there are few algorithms which can guide the researcher into making the ideal choices for a particular situation. However, many of these choices are allied quite closely to different philosophical positions, and an awareness of this can at least ensure that the different elements of a research design are consistent with each other.

In this section we shall describe five choices that are of particular significance. The first four relate fairly closely to the basic dichotomy between the use of positivist and social constructionist approaches, and the last is a debate located mainly within the positivist paradigm. These five choices are summarised in Figure 3.3 and are discussed below in a little more detail.

Researcher is independent	vs	Researcher is involved
Large samples	vs	Small numbers
Testing theories	vs	Generating theories
Experimental design	vs	Fieldwork methods
Verification	vs	Falsification

Figure 3.3 *Key choices of research design*

Involvement of researcher

The first choice is whether the researcher should remain distanced from, or get involved with, the material that is being researched. Clearly this choice stems from one's philosophical view about whether or not it is possible for the observer to remain independent from the phenomena being observed. The traditional assumption in science is that the researcher must maintain complete independence if there is to be any validity in the results produced, although more recently it has become evident in areas such as nuclear physics that this ideal is not always possible. For example, the very act of measuring the position of a sub-atomic particle is likely to affect its velocity.

In social sciences, where claims of researchers' independence are harder to sustain, there are those who have tried to turn this apparent 'problem' into a virtue. This is the tradition of *action research*. It assumes that any social phenomena are continually changing rather than static. Action research and the researcher are then seen as part of this change process itself. The following two features are normally part of action research projects:

1 a belief that the best way of learning about an organisation or social system is through attempting to change it, and this therefore should to some extent be the objective of the action researcher;
2 the belief that those people most likely to be affected by, or involved in implementing, these changes should as far as possible become involved in the research process itself.

Although it is possible to conduct action research in a positivist way, for example by attempting to change the organisation from the outside and then measuring the results, in most respects it derives from ideas that are alien to positivism. Many people schooled in positivist research methods are sceptical about the value of action research but, as Susman and Evered (1978) point out, action research is *bound* to be found wanting if it is measured against the criteria of positivist science; whereas it is perfectly justifiable from the viewpoint of other philosophies, such as phenomenology.

The involvement of the researcher is taken a stage further in what has come to be known as *cooperative inquiry* (Reason, 1988). This has been developed for researching human action more at an individual, rather than at organisational, levels. It adopts as a starting point the idea that all people have (at least latently) the ability to be self-directing, to choose how they will act and to give meaning to their own experiences. It rejects traditional positivist methods where people are studied as if they were objects under the influence of external forces. Cooperative inquiry not only focuses on the experiences and explanations of the individuals concerned, it also involves them in deciding in the first place what questions and issues are worth researching. Thus the subjects become partners in the research process.

Sampling
A second design choice is whether to attempt to sample across a large number of organisations or situations, or whether to focus on a small number of situations and attempt to investigate them over a period of time. This is essentially a choice between *cross-sectional* and *longitudinal design*.

Cross-sectional designs usually involve selecting different organisations, or units in different contexts, and investigating how other factors vary across these units. Thus to investigate the relationship between expenditure on management training and corporate performance one needs to select a sample of organisations that are known to represent either a range of levels in training investment *or* a range of levels of corporate performance. One then checks to see whether there is any correlation between the variables. A key problem here is in deciding how large the sample of organisations needs to be in order to be adequately representative. This is discussed further in Chapter 6, which considers the use of quantitative methods.

Cross-sectional designs, particularly where they use questionnaires and survey techniques, have the ability to describe economically features of large numbers of people or organisations. But two limitations are frequently evident. Firstly, they do not explain *why* correlations exist; and secondly, they have difficulty eliminating all the external factors which could possibly have caused the observed correlation.

Pettigrew (1985) suggests that longitudinal research, which focuses on a small number of organisations over long periods of time, can remedy these disadvantages. He recommends that research should focus on change processes within the broader social, economic and political context surrounding each organisation, and that it should gather 'time series data' over periods of time significantly longer than the immediate focus. In this way explanations should emerge from examining patterns in the process of change. The main practical advantage to this approach is that it can produce significant results from a very small number of cases and this can reduce the problems of gaining access if the research is to be carried out in organisations. The disadvantages are that it is extremely time consuming and the complexity of data requires very high skills from all researchers involved.

Theory and data
The third choice is about which should come first: the theory or the data. Again this represents the split between the positivist and phenomenological paradigms in relation to how the researcher should go about his or her work. In the latter case there is the approach known as *grounded theory*, which was first formulated in a classic book by Glaser and Strauss (1967).

Glaser and Strauss see the key task of the researcher as being to develop theory through 'comparative method'. This means looking at the same event or process in different settings or situations. For example, the researcher might be interested in the workings of appraisal interviews and would therefore study a number of appraisal interviews handled by different managers, in different departments, or in different organisations. As a result of the studies it might be noticed that most appraisal interviews either focus on reviewing performance and whether or not last year's objectives have been achieved, or focus on future goals and how the subordinate may be helped to achieve them. They might then be labelled as 'judgemental' or 'developmental' interviews, and the distinction would represent a *substantive theory* about appraisal interviews.

However, the theorising could be taken further. For example, it might be observed that neither form of interview has much effect on the individual's performance or on the relationships between the managers and their subordinates. Thus one might conclude that both forms of interview are simply organisational rituals which have the function of demonstrating and reinforcing hierarchical power relations. This would be the beginning of a more generalised *formal theory* about power and organisational rituals. Glaser and Strauss consider both kinds of theory to be valuable, and they propose two main criteria for evaluating the quality of a theory. Firstly it should be sufficiently *analytic* to enable some generalisation to take place, but at the same time it should be possible for people to relate the theory to their own experiences, thus *sensitising* their own perceptions.

The contrasting view is that one should start with a theory, or hypothesis, about the nature of the world, and then seek data that will confirm or disconfirm that theory. Thus, continuing with the above example, one might hypothesise that the prevalence of 'judgemental' or 'developmental' appraisal interviews depends on the personality of the boss, and that 'authoritarian' bosses will be more likely to conduct interviews in a judgemental manner. To test this hypothesis one needs to classify the bosses according to their authoritarian tendencies and to classify the appraisal interviews by type. If the data shows that most of the authoritarian bosses do indeed hold judgemental interviews then this will support the initial hypothesis. (We discuss in Chapter 6 methods and problems in interpreting statistical data such as this.)

The main practical advantage of the 'hypothesis testing' approach described above is that there is initial clarity about what is to be investigated, and hence information can be collected speedily and efficiently. Clarity of method means that it is easier for another researcher to replicate the study, and hence any claims arising from the research can be subjected to public scrutiny. The disadvantages are that its contribution may be quite trivial, confirming what is already known. And if the results are inconclusive or negative, the approach can give little guidance on why this is so. By contrast, the grounded approach is flexible and is good at providing both explanations and new insights. However it may take more time, and researchers often have to live with the fear that nothing of interest will emerge from the work. Some people regard grounded theory as suspect because of the lack of clarity and standardisation of methods, but that concern stems largely from a positivist perspective on the importance of 'finding the truth'.

Experimental designs or fieldwork

Experiments are one of the key elements of scientific method, although they are not necessarily essential to positivist methods. Classic experimental method involves assigning subjects *at random* to either an experimental or a control group. Conditions for the experimental group are then manipulated by the experimenter in order to assess their effect in comparison with members of the control group who are subjected to no unusual conditions. In studies of social and human life, such experiments still remain quite popular amongst psychologists, particularly where there is a ready supply of undergraduate students upon whom to conduct the experiments. They are very much harder to conduct within real organisations, or where there is no captive population from which to draw volunteers. Occasionally, if she is as lucky as Melville Dalton (1964) was, the researcher might find people who are prepared to set up small artificial experiments for her when she is studying within organisations, but this is obviously a rarity.

Some researchers still working from within the positivist paradigm recognised the practical difficulties of producing pure experimental designs, and thus the idea of 'quasi-experimental' designs was developed. The classic exposition of this is Campbell and Stanley (1963), where they evaluate a range of designs which make use of multiple measures over time in order to reduce the effects of control and experimental groups not being fully matched. One of the most common methods is the 'pre-test/post-test comparison design'. For example, the effects of a course on a group of managers might be evaluated by measuring the managers' knowledge or attitudes before and after the course, and by comparing the differences with those from a similar group of managers who did not attend the course but who completed identical tests at the same times. This design is illustrated in Figure 3.4 but the problems of using it in real organisations are substantial. For example, the design assumes that 'nothing' happens to the control group during the period that the treatment (course attendance) is being given to the experimental group. This is a naive assumption, as Mark found when attempting to evaluate a project-based management development programme held at Durham University Business School (Easterby-Smith and Ashton, 1975). While the

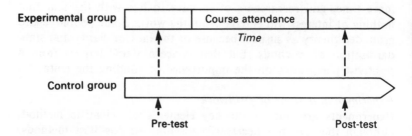

Figure 3.4 *Quasi-experimental research design*

'chosen few' were away on the course several members of the control group seized the opportunity to improve relationships with their bosses and strengthen their political standing in the company, thus effectively shutting out a number of managers who had attended the course.

The alternative to experimental and quasi-experimental designs is *fieldwork*, which is the study of real organisations or social settings. This may involve the use of positivist methods which use quantitative techniques, or it can be much more open-ended and phenomenological. One of the distinctive research styles in the latter case is *ethnography*. Here the researcher tries to immerse himself or herself in a setting and to become part of the group under study in order to understand the meanings and significances that people put upon their own behaviour and that of others.

Most outsiders who are new to an organisation or group will encounter things that they do not understand. These are what Agar (1986) calls 'breakdowns': events or situations where the researcher's past experience gives him no help in understanding what is going on. This breakdown therefore represents something unique about that organisation, and previously unknown to the researcher. For example, most groups have 'in-jokes', based on experiences shared only by members of the group. In order for an outsider to make sense of the breakdown provided by an 'in-joke' it will be necessary to track back to the original experiences. The breakdown provides a kind of window into exploring aspects of the experiences and meaning systems of groups and organisations. It will only be possible to resolve the breakdown when the researcher has understood these meaning systems. In this way the ethnographer is able to extend conventional wisdom, and to generate new insights into human behaviour.

Verification or falsification

The distinction between *verification* or *falsification* was made by Karl Popper (1959) as a way of dealing with what has become known as 'the problem of induction'. This is that, however much data one obtains in support of a scientific theory or law, it is not possible to reach a conclusive proof of the truth of that law. Popper's way out of this problem is to suggest that instead of looking for confirmatory evidence one should always look for evidence that will *disconfirm* one's hypothesis or existing view. This means that theories should be formulated in a way that will make them most easily exposed to possible refutation. The advantage then is that only one instance of refutation is needed to falsify a theory, whereas however many confirmations of the theory there are it will still not be conclusively proven.

The example often given to illustrate this approach takes as a start the assertion that all swans are white. If following the verification route, the researcher would start travelling around the country accumulating sightings of swans and, provided that he or she did not go near a zoo, a very high number of white sightings would eventually be obtained, and presumably no black sightings. This gives a lot of confidence to the assertion that all swans are white, but still does not conclusively prove the statement. If on the other hand, the researcher takes a falsification view, he or she would start to search for swans that are *not* white, deliberately looking for contexts and locations where non-white swans might be encountered. Thus, our intrepid researcher would head straight for a zoo, or perhaps book a flight to Australia, where most swans happen to be black. This discovery made, the initial hypothesis would be falsified, and it might then have to be modified to include the idea that all swans are either white or black. This statement has still what Popper calls high 'informative' content because it is expressed in a way that can easily be disproved; whereas a statement like 'all swans are large birds' would not be sufficiently precise to allow easy refutation.

Much of the debate about verification and falsification fits within the positivist view because ideas of 'truth' and 'proof' are associated mainly with that paradigm. But the phenomenologist might also take important lessons from this discussion. For example, Reason (1988) advocates 'critical subjectivity', which involves recognising one's own views and experiences, but not allowing oneself to be overwhelmed and swept along by them. If the idea of falsification is to be applied more fully to phenomenological research then one should look for evidence that might confirm or contradict what one currently believes to be true. This advice applies not only to researchers but also to managers who are concerned to investigate and understand what is taking place within their own organisations. According to this view it is important for them to resist the strong temptation to look for data that confirms whatever position they are currently holding. By deliberately searching for *disconfirmatory* evidence they may come up with answers much more quickly. If they find themselves unable to find such evidence this will make their current positions far stronger.

Criteria for choice
These five choices of research design are of course not absolute. People do use designs that incorporate both sides of the picture, and very often the choices that they make are not altogether 'pure'. However, given that time and resources are usually very limited in research, we feel that it is important that researchers are prepared to make choices and thereby provide a clear focus to their efforts. We have indicated some strengths and weaknesses of different design choices as we have progressed through the last section, and we assume that it will also be possible to detect our preference for the social constructionist view. However, we all have initial research training within more positivist traditions, and no doubt will find it necessary occasionally in the future to adopt methods informed by the positivist position. This suggests two possible criteria for choice of research design: the personal preference of the researchers themselves, and the aims or context of the research to be carried out.

A third criterion comes from a very common fear amongst researchers of all persuasions. The question asked is: will the research stand up to outside scrutiny and will anyone believe what I am saying about it? The technical language for examining this problem includes terms such as sampling theory, validity, reliability and generalisability. It should be no surprise by this stage to realise that the meaning of these terms varies considerably with the philosophical viewpoint adopted. Figure 3.5 summarises some of the differences from positivist and phenomenological viewpoints.

As Kirk and Miller (1986) point out, the language of validity and reliability was originally developed for use in quantitative social science, and many procedures have been devised for assessing different facets of each. There has been some reluctance to apply these ideas to phenomenological, and social constructionist, research because they might imply acceptance of one absolute (positivist) reality. However, provided the researcher is committed to providing a faithful description of others' understandings and

	Positivist viewpoint	Phenomenological viewpoint
Validity	Does an instrument measure what it is supposed to measure?	Has the researcher gained full access to the knowledge and meanings of informants?
Reliability	Will the measure yield the same results on different occasions (assuming no real change in what is to be measured)?	Will similar observations be made by different researchers on different occasions?
Generalis-ability	What is the probability that patterns observed in a sample will also be present in the wider population from which the sample is drawn?	How likely is it that ideas and theories generated in one setting will also apply in other settings?

Figure 3.5 *Questions of reliability, validity and generalisability*

perceptions, then ideas such as validity and reliability can provide a very useful discipline.

Research designs within different management subjects

In this final section of the chapter we will look briefly at the extent to which research methods are different in some of the key 'management' subject areas, such as finance and accounting, marketing, operational research, and organisational behaviour. As Morgan and Smircich (1980) observe, the appropriateness of a research approach 'derives from the nature of the social phenomena to be explored' (p. 491). Thus the extent to which the basic subject material in a discipline is quantified exerts a considerable influence on the preference of researchers for more positivist or phenomenological methods. Thus, within finance and accounting and operational research, it is inevitable that a lot of research will focus on measurable and quantifiable factors, and that the researcher remains as distanced as possible from the data or problems being tackled. It is also important to be aware of assumptions about what 'matters' when trying to understand or explain aspects of management and organisation. Is it the things themselves, or people's views about them, that are important? Researchers who incline towards the former view will tend to adopt a positivist framework, and those favouring the latter view will be happier with a social constructionist perspective.

One would expect the areas of operational research and management to be dominated by a concern with numbers and 'things'. But a number of well known people have deviated markedly from the straight and narrow, including Stafford Beer (1975), Reginald Revans (1982) and Peter Checkland (1981). The latter has achieved fame for developing a 'soft systems' methodology which adopts a holistic approach – using concepts rather than numbers – to understand the complexity of organisational problems. The methodology provides a systematic way of inquiring into the nature of the world, but in no way assumes that the world itself is, or can be described by a system. Thus the methodology has far more in common with phenomenology than with positivism.

Similar examples of non-positivist research exist in the field of finance and accounting. For example, much interesting work is now being conducted around the relationship between human behaviour and financial systems. Share price movements seem to be determined less by objective economic indicators than by psychological factors (or at least by the way these economic indicators are interpreted by people); there is also a lot of interest in the way that firms exercise discretion in disclosing information and about the processes of interpretation of their own data. There has also been significant growth over the last decade in the area of 'behavioural accounting' which essentially tries to understand the effect of different accounting and control systems on people, and vice versa. In a recent review of research methods in this field, Brownell and Trotman (1988) comment that different kinds of research questions should be investigated with different methodologies. They observe, however, that most research in this area has used either experimental methods or survey techniques. In their view the greater use of methods such as quasi-experiments and participant observation would lead to much richer understanding.

Hirschman (1986) argues that the key factors in marketing are essentially socially constructed: human beliefs, behaviours, perceptions and values. Hence it is important to employ research methods drawn from this perspective, such as observation and qualitative interviews. But academics within the marketing field still show a strong preference for survey research methods, which are aimed at predicting, often statistically, behaviour amongst consumers or clients. This may be because marketing as an academic discipline has emerged from economics and the behavioural sciences, and both of these have well established quantitative traditions. On the other hand commercial market research agencies rely heavily on qualitative methods. As Jobber and Horgan's (1987) study into the actual practices of agencies revealed, skills in interviewing and personal communication were considered to be more valuable than mastery of statistical techniques. Despite both changes in the concept of marketing and actual commercial practices, the teaching of market research still retains a heavy bias towards quantitative rather than qualitative approaches.

Finally, there is the field of organisational behaviour. Here, again, the traditional methods in the subject have been closer to the quantitative and positivist paradigm, with studies such as the research at Aston University which we have described above being of particular significance. Despite some disillusionment about the value of positivist methods in this field, many researchers simply respond by redoubling their efforts. For example, White and Mitchell (1976), after reviewing the indifferent results produced by 67 different studies of the effect of organisation development (OD) interventions, conclude: 'To generate a comprehensive theory of OD, practitioners and researchers should increase the sophistication of the research designs, methodology, and statistics currently in use' (p. 70). But there are many others who advocate the use of qualitative methods which originate from a non-positivist perspective (Silverman, 1970; Pettigrew, 1985; Walker, 1985), and it seems that this trend will continue.

Conclusions

In this chapter we have discussed some of the key philosophical debates underlying research methods in the social sciences, and we have looked at the implications these have for the design of management research. Although there is a clear dichotomy between the positivist and social constructionist world views, and sharp differences of opinion exist between researchers about the desirability of methods, the reality of research also involves a lot of compromises between these pure positions.

The world view held by an individual researcher or institute is clearly an important factor in the choice of research methods. But there are other factors, too. Within academic organisations senior members can exert pressure on junior people to adopt methods that they don't believe in. Governments, companies and funding organisations can exert pressure on institutions to ensure that the aims and forms of research meet with their interests. The politics of research are complex, and researchers neglect them at their peril. That is why we have chosen to devote the next chapter to a discussion of these issues.

4
The Politics of Management Research

One of the myths about research is that it is an ivory tower activity. According to this view, research is carried out by independent scholars dedicated to the pursuit of knowledge. Questions and issues are defined as interesting according to the current state of knowledge and the curiosity of the researcher's intellect.

It is doubtful whether there was ever much truth behind this myth. Scholars have regularly got themselves into trouble for following beliefs that were politically unpopular. Socrates was condemned to drink a cup of hemlock because he did not seem sufficiently respectful of current Athenian divinities; and Galileo was forced to recant his belief, based on careful observation of sunspots and planetary orbits, that the earth moved around the sun. In China the first Qin emperor is reputed to have buried alive some 400 scholars because he did not like their opinions, and evidently intellectuals continue to have their problems there more than 2,000 years later.

Although many academics have tried in the past to maintain their independence it has never been altogether possible to separate scholarship from politics. And this is at least as true today, as Punch (1986) comments with regard to social research: to a greater or lesser extent, 'politics' suffuses all sociological research (p. 13).

This comment provides a good starting point for considering the politics of management research. We see 'politics' as concerning the power relationships between the individuals and institutions involved in the research enterprise; it includes the strategies adopted by different actors and the consequences of their actions on others. The crucial relationships may be between student and supervisor, funder and grant holder, authors and journal editors, companies and research institutes, project leaders and research assistants, researchers and managers, or between managers and their bosses. Amongst these actors influence may be exerted over: what is to be researched, how, when, by whom; how information is to be used and disseminated; and how the products of research are to be evaluated.

In this context it is important to emphasise two major features of management research. Firstly, 'management' is essentially about controlling, influencing and structuring the awareness of others. It is the central process whereby organisations achieve the semblance of coherence and direction. This process is increasingly recognised as being political (Mintzberg, 1973; Lee and Piper, 1986). Although 'management' is not the only arena in which politics is important, it does mean that political issues will rarely be far removed from the research process.

The second difference is linked, and it starts with the observation that most empirical research in the social sciences is carried out on members of society who are less powerful than the researchers. That is why psychologists conduct their experiments on students rather than on professors, and sociologists tend to focus on people who are relatively powerless due to their low social or economic status (Taylor and Bogdan, 1984). It is 'the mad, the bad, and the ill' who have received most attention from social researchers in the past (Slater, 1989). This is no accident, however, for the more powerful members of society generally have both the awareness and the means to protect themselves from the prying eyes and tape recorders of researchers. It is rare to find researchers who have succeeded in studying powerful members of society without adopting methods of deceit, concealment or subterfuge. This, particularly in the case of 'conflict methodology', raises some major ethical dilemmas which will be discussed later in this chapter.

Research into managers and management provides a case where the subjects of research are very likely to be more powerful than the researchers themselves. Furthermore, most managers are to be found within organisations that are fairly tightly structured and controlled. Gaining access to the corporate board room is exceedingly difficult for researchers. Most managers are in a position where they can easily decline to provide information for researchers; they are also adept at handling face-to-face interviews and at managing interaction with strangers. Managers, especially senior ones, spend a lot of their time handling relations with colleagues and with competitors and other external bodies. In such circumstances they are only too aware of the significance of information and the importance of determining what use it might be put to, and by whom. So, in the case of managerial research the boot is on the other foot. The determination of what can be researched, or is worth researching, (the research question) is by no means straightforward.

We therefore begin this chapter with a discussion of the way the nature and direction of research may be shaped by contextual factors and by different people who feel they have a right to exert their influence. The next part of the chapter focuses on some of the problems and ethical dilemmas that researchers may face in the course of conducting fieldwork, and the final part looks at the problems of utilisation.

Factors that may influence the research question

Researchers are not keen on self-disclosure, and they rarely explain precisely where their ideas and questions have come from. The conventional (positivist) view of scientific, and social scientific, method is that one should review the existing literature and research findings, identify some gaps and inconsistencies in the state of the art, and then design experiments or collect data that will enable existing ideas to be tested further, or cover evident gaps in knowledge and theory.

Fortunately, as we have shown above, a number of studies have been carried out on how real researchers go about their business. It is now clear that some of the most significant advances come about haphazardly, rather than through steady accumulation of data and evidence. A classic example from science is Einstein's theory of relativity, which was based on hunches about data that had been known to scientists for at least 50 years before his time.

Einstein also had a very well prepared mind based on long acquaintance with this data. This principle applies equally well to social research, where deep and sustained involvement with particular settings and organisations has often led to new insights, ideas and questions. The ideas of Frederick Taylor (1947) have aroused great controversy and are frequently dismissed nowadays for their naivety; but there is no denying their impact on industrial practice over the last hundred years. It was Taylor's experience at the Midvale Steel Company, first as a labourer, and then as a foreman in the 1880s, which showed him how working practices could be used to restrict output. This led him to focus his attention on the way people worked, from which he developed the idea of scientific management.

Dalton's (1959) study of managerial behaviour is very important because it shows the differences between the formal and informal aspects of power and influence within American companies. His insights were based on extensive experience as a manager at Milo, and through direct contact with a network of surrounding companies.

These examples show the importance of interaction between the *researcher* and the *subject of study*. Pettigrew (1985) points out that research ideas usually evolve in an incremental way through a continual process of negotiation – and he sees this as a justification for longitudinal studies. Negotiation also needs to take place with those who may use, or be affected by, the results of a particular study. Taylor's 'scientific management' was very useful for managers, but very unpopular with the workers on whom it was applied. The interests of such people – whom we call *stakeholders* – are becoming increasingly important when considering both the applications of research as well as its conduct.

Stakeholders may have strong views about appropriate subjects of study, especially if those involved adopt a 'co-researcher' approach. And as we have noted above, stakeholders may be able to exert influence directly on the researchers themselves. In a later part of this chapter we will consider the problems and ethical issues concerned with those who may be seen as the 'victims' of research: those who have relatively little opportunity to influence its nature and direction, but whose interests may be adversely affected by its results. But for the time being we shall consider how to handle relationships with those who can exert influence – and given the increasing emphasis on 'value for money' in research it would appear that their influence is becoming increasingly significant.

As a basis for examining such relationships we have found the work of Boissevain (1974) to be particularly useful. Through studying, initially, the Sicilian mafiosi, he identified two key roles played by participants in social networks. They are Brokers and Patrons. Brokers are social 'fixers' who use their secondary resources, such as information and a wide range of contacts, in order to achieve their ambitions. Patrons are people with direct control over primary resources such as people and money. The interesting thing is that one cannot function effectively without the other.

Brokers build their reputations in various networks by creating a kind of social credit based on a history of previous successful deals with Patrons. The nature of the social network according to Boissevain is as follows. A Patron has funds and resources he can commit in exchange for information or the resolution of a problem. The Broker over a period of time will have gained respect and social credit in the eyes of the Patron and the deal goes ahead.

While we would not wish to suggest a direct correspondence between the worlds of mafiosi and management researchers, there are a number of parallels. In the research world brokers are important because they know the way round the system, and are known by others. They may be able to advise on questions such as: how to obtain funds from Research Councils; which external examiners would be most appropriate for a thesis; which journal editor is most likely to be interested in a particular paper; which people are

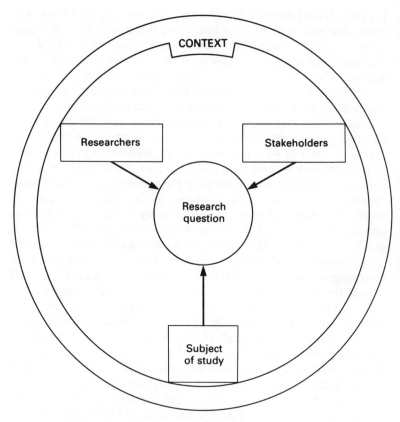

Figure 4.1   *Influences on the research question*

able to grant access to a particular organisation. Brokers are to be found in the academic world and in organisations.

Personnel and training managers frequently act as Brokers because, although they have little formal power, they usually have a wide range of contacts at all levels of the organisation which can give them additional influence. Thus they are often the best people to arrange access for researchers to an organisation because of their influence with senior managers who are able to provide authorisation. In this case they are also fulfilling the function of 'gatekeepers'. Successful researchers can also develop 'brokerage' skills. Thus a personnel manager is more likely to help provide access to her company if she thinks the researcher may be able to provide her with something in return – whether it be experience, credibility or other contacts.

All of this will take place within a wider *context*. For example, research may be carried out from a university base, or from a company or consultancy organisation; it may take place in a setting where there are plentiful funds and resources, or where there are virtually no computers and anyway the electricity supply cannot be guaranteed for more than four hours at a time.

In this section we argue that the focus of management research will usually emerge from a process of negotiation between these three elements – researchers, stakeholders and subject – all within the constraints of the wider context. These features are illustrated in Figure 4.1, and on the following pages we elaborate on the nature and effects of each feature.

The researcher
The research may be carried out by an individual or a number of individuals. They may be students, paid researchers, academic teachers, or managers and others working within organisations. In this respect we have noticed trends over the last few years. One is the increasing practice of students working in groups to conduct research projects (particularly for taught Masters' degrees), where hitherto the tradition was for students to work entirely on their own. The second trend is for managers themselves to take a greater role in conducting pieces of research within their own organisa-tions, either as a way of helping themselves to make decisions or as a basis for encouraging others to change.

The motivations of individual researchers may be quite varied. As Platt (1976) has shown, many researchers in the early stages of projects are unclear about their aims and goals; others may have more precisely defined career goals, political aims, or agendas to create change in their own institutions and environments. In most cases researchers prefer to investigate settings and people with whom they have some affinity. Those who conduct research on workers rarely get round to investigating managers, and vice versa. This may be for ideological reasons, or merely for personal and social ease. Most organisations are highly sensitive to the possibility of researchers having any kind of political agenda, particularly if it differs from theirs. Amusingly, Beynon (1988) recounts problems that he and his colleagues have encountered in gaining access both to what he regarded as a 'right-wing' manufac-turing organisation, *and* to a 'left-wing' trade union organisation.

So how does the nature of the researcher influence the research question? Firstly, past experience is likely to determine what the researcher is interested in, and also his or her ability to identify phenomena and questions as being significant. In particular, as we have noted in the previous chapter, the world view held by the researcher may exert a strong influence on what is seen to be important. And when it comes to fieldwork, personal background, including social class, will affect the ease with which the researcher can gain access to different settings, and this may also predetermine responses from different client groups.

Many of the points we have made here about individual researchers can be applied to the case of research teams. There are several advantages to be gained from working in teams, especially the possibility of combining people with different backgrounds and interests, and the flexibility and synergy that this can create. But there may also be problems to do with leadership and decision-making; and in the case of funded research projects additional problems can arise from the structure of the academic research profession.

For example, Hyder and Sims (1979) consider that one of the main reasons for the non-completion of many projects is the traditional distinction between 'grant holders', who are awarded the funds, and 'research officers', who are hired to carry out the work. They suggest that there are three main aspects to this problem. Firstly, there is a contradiction between the research project which is conceived by the grant holder as a long term project, and the chronic insecurity of research officers who are invariably hired on short term contracts. Secondly, working on a research project is essentially a lonely and isolated activity. There may be limited contact between the researcher and grant holder, because the latter will have many other responsibilities and commitments, and there are unlikely to be other researchers working in related areas. Thirdly, most grant holders develop conflicting expectations of their research officers, expecting them on the one hand to be general factotums and dogsbodies, and on the other to be creative contributors to the research enterprise.

Barwise et al. (1989) also encountered the latter issue in the context of a multidisciplinary investigation of strategic investment decisions. Although the project was conceived and 'sold' to the grant-giving body by three senior staff, it was carried out by a half-time researcher who was recruited for this purpose. The senior academics initially treated the researcher as their 'eyes and ears', but about halfway through the project they were forced to recognise that she had developed a greater understanding of the project than they, and that she now had a major contribution to make both in the interpretation of data and in the overall direction of the project.

There is much potential for conflict here. The power of grant holders lies in their control of funds and their potential influence on the future career of the researcher; the researcher's power lies in intimate knowledge of the research process and the potential to withhold cooperation. Thus both parties are in a position to exert influence on the appropriate focus throughout the project, although the relative balance of this might vary as the project evolves.

The stakeholders

We use the term 'stakeholders' here in a broad sense to include anybody who may feel they have a legitimate claim to influence the nature and direction of the research. The two main groups of stakeholders are those in the academic community (including supervisors or colleagues working in similar fields), and those in the organisational or commercial community. Each of these is in a position to influence in some ways both the nature of questions that are seen as worthwhile to investigate, and the methods of investigating them.

The academic community   The first of the two main stakeholders is the 'academic community', which exerts much influence on the direction of research through control of funds, accreditation and career rewards. Academic funding bodies frequently come under government pressure to demonstrate their relevance to the national economy, which means that they are likely to favour projects that have fairly clear applications.

A reasonable amount of responsiveness to national, social and economic needs may well be a good thing. Research Councils in a number of countries have now adopted policies of targeting resources towards specific initiatives which may generate sufficient critical mass to provide rapid development of theories and practical applications. But there is also a danger if funding becomes *too* responsive to political priorities and pressures. In such circumstances research may be used by one group directly to harm another group, and it is very easy for researchers to become compromised in the process. An extreme example of this is the work carried out by scientists in Nazi Germany on concentration camp inmates. The majority of those involved appeared to be highly principled, as scientists, and strongly denied any anti-semitism. Yet in a review of a careful study of surviving evidence, Billig (1988) comments: 'In *Murderous Science*, we see academics continually writing grant applications, guessing what projects the controllers of the funding agencies will be considering socially useful: is it the Gypsies, or the degenerates; or the ability to withstand cold, which will bring the grants this year? (p. 476). He who pays the piper not only calls the tune, but can also define what a good tune is. One hopes that exercises such as these would never take place in or around modern organisations. But the personal and social consequences of losing a power struggle, or a job, can be very profound indeed. Researchers should therefore be very wary of the ends that they may be serving, whether wittingly or unwittingly.

Those seeking funds from grant-giving bodies should be aware that many proposals are received which are technically sound. Thus decisions about the award of funds often have to take other information into account. Chief among these are whether the researcher has a good 'track record' and whether he or she is known to those involved in making the decision. For those with international reputations and many years' successful research experience, this is an advantage; but for the newcomer it can create a major obstacle to getting started on funded research.

For newcomers we can offer three main pieces of advice. Firstly, make the best use of your own experience by highlighting any related work you have done, especially if it has been published. It is also important to be able to show that you have a record of delivering according to your promises. Secondly, get known by key people in the field by going to conferences and submitting papers for publication. Thirdly, make use of networks, possibly by submitting proposals jointly with people who are already established, and by sending drafts to potential referees. In effect the research grant applicants must demonstrate their credibility as brokers who will ensure that the work will be completed to the full satisfaction of the funding agency.

However, it is worth noting that once funds have been allocated the influence of research-funders becomes less. Control is then exercised mainly through monitoring budgets and checking that research outputs correspond with the promises made in the original proposal. It is rare for the funder to attempt to monitor the content, direction or process of research activities (Barwise et al. 1989).

For those working on projects or research degrees, other academic pressures come from supervisors, from colleagues and from 'gatekeepers'. Supervisors, for example, will normally try to influence the research so that it stays fairly close in terms of both content and methodology to their own research interests. If the research is being conducted for a PhD or Masters' degree, the supervisor will be increasingly anxious about whether the work will be completed successfully within a given time (currently 4 years is the magic deadline for PhDs in the UK); this is because both academic departments and whole institutions are now being judged quite drastically upon completion rates for research students. The consequence of this is that both institutions and supervisors are tending to push students into limiting the scope of their research topics so that they are easily completed within the prescribed time, and hence the PhD in the UK is becoming closer to that in the USA: a 'research training' rather than a major piece of original work.

The nature and direction of research can be influenced by other forces, too. Most academic departments have their own house styles which support and encourage particular kinds of work, whether quantitative or qualitative, and there is also much pressure on departments to prioritise their research interests and to narrow their scope. For people working on research degrees there is always the problem of being able to find appropriate external examiners. This is not easy sometimes because the ideal external examiner not only needs to share the same research philosophy as the candidate, but also needs to know a lot about the subject of investigation – without becoming too defensive if the findings of the research happen to disagree with his or her own work. In this case the supervisor should normally act as broker, with the external examiner who has effective power to award or withhold the degree, as patron. It is advisable in most cases to start looking for potential external examiners at a fairly early stage in a research degree. This not only helps to focus the research project, but should also allow time to become familiar with the publications and opinions of the person who will be the judge of the thesis.

Conferences, as we have mentioned above, are a useful source of contact within the academic community. Sometimes they can be used to sound out potential external examiners, and presenting papers at conferences can provide valuable feedback and visibility for one's ideas. Conferences are often published as books or in the form of proceedings. In order to develop an academic career it is essential to publish in these proceedings, or in journals. It is therefore hardly surprising that people who edit journals play a crucial gatekeeping role. Both conferences and journals have distinctive ideologies and house styles. Articles that would be welcomed with open arms by one prestigious journal would be rejected out of hand by another. It is important to understand the preferences of these organs and their editors, and this can be done most easily by reading back numbers of relevant journals or by contacting their editors. There are also significant national differences in preferred publication style. Although the USA dominates management publications through sheer volume, a number of good European journals have developed along very distinct lines. American authors now have difficulty getting published in these journals because they have been trained to write in a style that is not appreciated in Europe – and vice versa.

Commercial sponsors   The second important group of clients are those in the organisations being studied. Here there is a marked conflict in the literature between people who focus their research on management and those who conduct more general research into organisations. The conflict hinges on whether they see the potential influence of organisational members as an irritant to be circumvented, or as a significant contributor to the research process itself. Writers such as Bulmer (1988), Beynon (1988) and Dalton (1964) take the former, more purist, view. Reason and Rowan (1981) and Buchanan et al. (1988) take the latter view, arguing that the quality of research insights will be enhanced if members can influence what takes place.

Earlier in this chapter we distinguished between brokers and patrons on the grounds that the former (as gatekeepers) control access to the organisation, and the latter control resources. But in some respects the role and influence of the two groups is not very different, because both are involved in making commitments on behalf of the organisation. Thus the distinction may be primarily one of different *degrees* of interest.

Buchanan et al. (1988) discuss in some detail the problems of gaining access to organisations and argue for an opportunistic approach. They also recommend making informal contacts, through people in the middle of the organisation, such as personnel and training people, rather than trying to make a formal approach to the top of the organisation. It is important to remember that gatekeepers will rarely provide a researcher with access purely for the love of science and knowledge. Many organisations, particularly those that are in any way seen to be 'leading' in a field, receive repeated requests from researchers to be allowed access. Unless one can make use of networks, or unless the research is clearly felt to be in the interests of the gatekeeper, the chances are that he will not be prepared to commit that most valuable resource: his time.

In our experience it is most important to have the right contact (and it is usually better for this person to be a broker than a patron). It is usually possible to identify such people by talking to relevant trade or professional associations, or using contacts in related organisations. We have found associations to be very helpful here, and they rarely object to being mentioned as the source of the contact – because, of course, brokerage is the lifeblood of most trade and professional associations.

Once the initial contact has been made, by phone or letter, the gatekeeper is likely to consider two questions: (a) is this individual worth supporting, and (b) will it be possible to 'sell' the project to patrons higher up the organisation? The latter question hangs on a consideration of whether the potential benefits will outweigh the likely costs, or potential risks, of the project. Given that information about costs and benefits will be very imprecise it usually helps at this stage if:

1 the time and resources requested are minimal;
2 the project appears not to be politically sensitive; and
3 the individuals concerned, and their institution, have a good reputation.

Two recent examples at Lancaster can illustrate these points, both being projects funded by the Economic and Social Research Council (ESRC). The first project aimed to examine the relationship between management development policy and corporate performance in 60 major UK companies over a 15-year period. The methodology required analysis of financial indicators over this period (from public databases), and interviews with up to 5 key actors in each company. Gaining access to the latter was relatively easy since the research question was seen to be important and we were not asking for much ('an initial interview of 1 hour with a senior personnel manager, with the possibility of a small number of other interviews subsequently'). Consequently, we only had to approach 83 companies in order to reach our final sample of 49.

It should, however, be noted that access was much easier when we had a 'warm' contact: someone who already knew us. The success rates were somewhat lower with cold contacts. In almost every case it was necessary to be persistent. Three or four phone calls might be necessary before access would be given.

What is important here is that in many cases the person we approached, the personnel manager, was also in a position to grant what we required, an interview – and in this way the roles of broker and patron were combined.

The other example was less successful. This involved trying to gain access to British Steel for a research project comparing decision-making processes in Chinese and UK organisations. British Steel was important to us because several of the potential Chinese companies were large steel manufacturers. We pursued British Steel over a period of about two years and gradually collected a network of supporters first amongst central training staff, and then amongst senior line managers in operating companies. We were asking for access for about a week for 2 researchers (one Chinese and one

British), who would carry out about ten interviews in connection with two major decisions. Unfortunately, because of the potential political implications none of our brokers was in a position to act as a patron and commit the organisation. The decision was referred to Main Board level and an unequivocal letter of rejection followed shortly.

We never established exactly why we had failed to get into British Steel. The initial reason was that the company was in the process of privatisation and hence it would be inappropriate to grant access to outsiders at that time. Perhaps China was not seen as 'flavour of the month' then. But also we suspect that British Steel could not see how contacts with academics, or with the Chinese, were in its interests. Certainly the UK companies to which we subsequently gained access (the sample of Chinese companies had to be adjusted to match the changed profile of UK companies) had very clear ideas about what they wanted to gain from the project. These included identifying market opportunities, establishing contact with potential business partners, and obtaining information on the company's own image in China. Admittedly these concerns are recognised as being 'extras' to the main focus of the project, although several companies, especially the Chinese ones, showed an interest in direct involvement with the project.

There is a principle of reciprocity evident in the above examples. The more the company gives, in time or money, the more it expects in exchange. Another feature that is common to the above examples is that the initiative usually comes from the researcher, and organisational brokers may then be used to reach the patrons. However there are occasions when patrons themselves may wish to initiate some research, often as thinly veiled consultancy. At least five reasons for sponsoring research are common.

Firstly, the sponsor may wish to gain political support for a new idea that he wants to initiate. The mere presence of an outside adviser, or researcher, may lend credibility to this idea, and preliminary data produced by the researcher may lend further support. Secondly, the sponsor may wish to demonstrate, largely to an internal audience, the success of a venture with which he has been associated. This is a common reason for sponsoring evaluations of training or development programmes. The third reason is that the potential sponsor or his unit is under attack from others in the organisation. When a department or project is under threat of closure a possible line of defence is to introduce a researcher who can demonstrate how valuable the unit's work is. In our experience this stratagem rarely works. And the researcher must hope that the unit is not closed before he gets paid! Fourthly, the sponsor may simply wish to test his ideas against some external validation, by using the researcher as a sounding board. Finally, there are a few enlightened sponsors who are sufficiently curious about the world they work in to support research for its own sake.

Very often it may be a mix of these five reasons. But whichever it is, it is worth remembering that the very act of patronage, or brokerage, may itself be a clear demonstration of the power of the individual within the organisation; one manager said to us in a recent study: 'Any middle manager here can have his own secretary, but you really have to be quite important if you are to have your own personal consultant.'

The possibility that the client will have preferred outcomes from the study returns us to the issue of whether research will automatically become 'contaminated' by such political considerations. If this happens, some people argue, the results will be valueless, and therefore this kind of research should be avoided. Our view, however, and that of Buchanan et al. (1988), is that this kind of contamination is unavoidable in social research, especially when it is conducted within the management levels of an organisation.

The question then is not how to avoid 'contamination', but how best to deal with political influences on the research. The key point here is to regard these aspects as part of the research itself, and not as irritants that are best swept under the carpet. The researcher's own interests, the process of gaining access or funds from organisations, or discussions about dissemination of results: these may all be relevant. Thus we would advise all researchers to keep regular records not only of formal research 'data', but also to chronicle their own views and moods, and the processes of organising and conducting the research. Further, we think it important that researchers are prepared to reflect critically on all of those influences on their research, and to make these thoughts available to others. Ultimately this should increase, rather than decrease, the credibility of the results.

The subject of study

The general subject or topic of study may also exert considerable influence on the nature and direction of the research enterprise. By the 'subject' we mean the problems or issues to be considered – rather than the people and data that will be looked at within the study.

At the end of the last chapter we considered how different subjects can influence ways of conducting research; here we consider how subjects or disciplines can influence what are considered to be worthwhile research questions. Each academic discipline, whether it be mathematics, engineering, sociology or organisational theory, tends to have a number of key debates and issues at any one time. These debates are conducted by individuals and groups through the medium of publications and conferences, and frequently through the control of real resources, such as academic promotions and research grants. One can only get an idea of what these main debates are by talking to people, attending conferences, and by reading between the lines of the debates that occur in the academic journals. The ambitious researcher would be advised to attempt to locate his or her work fairly close to what is currently seen to be an important debate – provided there is some confidence that the same debate will still be around when the results of the research are likely to be produced! Those who locate their research efforts away from the mainstream of current debates may find their lives much quieter, but they are also likely to become isolated in the academic backwaters.

Despite the relevance of this advice to the individual researcher, it does raise a problem of more general relevance to research as a whole. There is a marked tendency amongst researchers to follow fads and fashions with regard to both method and focus.

For example, some of the fashionable debates stimulated by academic management researchers in the early 1990s are: post modernism, ethics and (critiques of) enterprise culture. A strong research emphasis on a limited number of areas such as these has obvious benefits in providing insights quickly, and in some depth. But it may result in other important or 'ordinary' issues being overlooked because they are out of fashion. Very often it is the ordinary and commonplace that can be most revealing. Ryave and Schenkein (1974), for example, describe a study of the relatively trivial topic of how people walk. Their results show how a number of social rules can be identified – with regard to space, control and propriety – which are by no means mundane, and which can easily be related to other contexts.

As we have indicated above, it is very likely that influential members of the organisation will also have clear views about the appropriate subject of investigation. In our experience it is advisable for the researcher to attempt to accommodate himself or herself to these expectations; they can often represent more of an opportunity than a problem. This dilemma of different academic and practical expectations is often encountered within collaborative research projects involving both academic and industrial sponsorship. One recent scheme of the ESRC provided funds for doctoral students whose projects were defined and supervised jointly by a sponsor from academia and one from a company. In some cases it was difficult to establish sufficient common purpose between the two perspectives, and the scheme was eventually discontinued.

However, there were plenty of examples of the appropriate combination being achieved. One research student was asked by her sponsoring company to investigate how appraisal systems were working in practice in different parts of the company. The researcher was able to answer this practical question to the satisfaction of the company. At the same time she was able to use data from her interviews to show how organisational systems, such as appraisals, are a product of wider cultural value systems in those parts of the organisation; and conversely how such systems are a channel for the transmission and articulation of value systems, particularly as defined by senior members of the organisation.

Thus there is no particular reason why academic and practical goals should not be achieved simultaneously; indeed we have also found that many practitioners will become enthusiastically involved in theoretical debates created from the academic perspective. Despite an unpromising start (Handy, et al. 1988), the educational background of managers in some of Britain's leading companies is now becoming quite high, and the rapid growth of company-based MBA programmes will contribute further. Such managers are not only likely to be familiar with academic debates about culture and values; they may also wish to contribute substantially to these debates. This increasingly leads to the possibility of managers, sponsors and gatekeepers being seen as collaborators in the research process itself or, as Reason and Rowan (1981) put it, as co-researchers.

The contexts and models of research

We have discussed research up to this point as if it was independent of the context within which it takes place, and that provided one can obtain access and cooperation the availability of the appropriate resources is largely immaterial. Increasingly, however, people who have conducted research in different cultural or national contexts have pointed out just how important the context is in constraining what is possible, and what is desirable.

Hickson (1988) provides a nice description of the contrasting resources for his research in oil-rich Alberta, and at the University of Bradford, which was at that time reeling from severe government cutbacks. Also, for the modern British researcher, Pugh's (1988) account of the early period of the Aston research programme sounds like a totally different world. He and his team were able to spend a whole year reading books and discussing what the focus of their research would be, without any expectation that they should rush off and gather data or produce preliminary reports within the first year of their work. Similarly, from another country, Davila (1989) argues that North American models of research which require large samples and substantial data analysis are largely irrelevant both methodologically and substantively in the context of Latin America. He advocates paying far more attention to case studies, which can draw more extensively upon local culture and problems – many of these problems being quite different from those considered significant in more highly developed countries.

Thus we believe that it is important for the researcher to be at least aware of the constraints and opportunities posed by the *context* within which he or she is currently working. This leads us to propose four archetypal research models, which, although they are not comprehensive, do at least demonstrate the diversity of what is possible and feasible. The first is what we call the *military model*, which involves: teams of people; substantial preparation and planning; some differentiation of roles between those who design the research, those who gather data, and those who make sense of the data; and substantial resources for the analysis and dissemination of the research findings. Typical examples of this style of research would be the work of Pugh and his colleagues at Aston, or of Hickson and his colleagues in Alberta. We have also noted above some of the problems that can be created by teams that contain hierarchies of roles.

Whereas in the military model the workers are generally hired for the job, with the second model, that of the *private agent*, one is more likely to encounter students and maverick academics. This involves individuals operating independently, developing their own ideas using their own resources, and making the best of whatever opportunities are available. Occasionally there may be an element of coordination, or networking, amongst the 'private agent' researchers, provided by a charismatic supervisor with a number of students. Institutions that run doctoral programmes may also establish arrangements whereby students, although conducting their research quite independently, are also members of action learning sets that provide support and guidance to each other. There is also a growing tendency among lone researchers to network electronically between institutions through media such as computer conferencing, and this allows sufficient critical mass to be achieved among a distributed population of 'private agent' researchers.

A third model of research which has received quite a lot of discussion and some opprobrium is the *investigative journalism* model. This starts from the assumption that powerful organisations and individuals will always try to control and repress research conducted on them, and hence if worthwhile research is to be carried out in these settings deception is legitimate and necessary. This implies that researchers should be opportunistic, they should use any means necessary to gain access and gather data, and they should publish their findings quickly regardless of consequences. One of the main proponents of this model – sometimes known as 'conflict methodology' – is Douglas (1976). Beynon's classic study of life on and around the assembly line at the Ford plant in Liverpool also had elements of investigative journalism in it (Beynon, 1973). But this subsequently attracted the comment from the company that: 'It's extreme left-wing propaganda . . . we don't think it merits serious discussion as it's not a serious attempt at sociology or education.' Many see this as strong corroboration of the findings in the book. But the method is controversial within the research community because of the backlash created by such tactics. Investigative researchers do a considerable service in terms of exposing fraud, injustices, the misuse of power, and organisational myths, but they may also damage the opportunities of future researchers to gain access to organisations – which would enable them to make their own names in their profession.

The fourth research model is what we might call an *appropriate technology* model. This is most useful in situations where the normal trappings of the research environment such as computers, photocopiers, easy communications and transport cannot be taken for granted. Increasingly, developing countries are appreciating the need for management practices which are based upon indigenous research. In these cases research methods must adjust to the realities of the developing country's situation, and they should not appear to be inferior in comparison to those of the far more munificent environments of developed countries.

All four of these models to some extent predetermine the kind of research questions that can, and should, be investigated in their respective cases. Thus one might expect grand theoretical issues to emerge from the military model; the private agent to focus on detailed and small scale processes and issues; the investigative journalism researcher to concentrate on exposing wrongdoings; and the appropriate technology researcher to use ethnographic methods to identify the actual processes of management or managing within the particular cultural context.

Politics and ethics

Buchanan et al. (1988), in describing the practicalities of field research, refer to the central phase of research work as 'getting on'. In other words, once one has gained some kind of access to an organisation, the next problem is to obtain cooperation and trust inside. Getting on within an organisation is largely a function of the personality of the researcher, and whether he or she is genuinely curious to find out what is happening; it is also a function of the researcher's skills in dealing with what are sometimes very complex interpersonal relationships.

In our experience these complex interpersonal relationships derive largely from the political issues within the organisation, and we divide these into micro-issues, that are to do with relationships between individual managers, and macro-issues which are to do with the wider political conflicts within the organisation. At a *micro-political* level the main problem is in not unwittingly divulging information to one individual when it was given in confidence by another. This may have very serious consequences where hierarchies are involved, and the researcher has to exercise the utmost care in not damaging the interests of informants. Informants who are politically adept often read a great deal into the question that the interviewer is asking. For example, on one occasion Mark was interviewing the Director of a national investigatory organisation about the longer term effects of a particular management development programme. He asked a carefully focused question about how the reward system was working, to which the Director immediately came back with: 'I take it you have been talking to John Dawson about that; well, in that case . . . .' Even though they may not be trained as investigators, managers will often be able to work out the nature and sources of information already collected by researchers who are sufficiently unfamiliar with the detailed political context of the organisation to be aware of the significance of the questions that they are asking.

This incident is a variant on the 'put down' technique often used by senior managers on hapless researchers. At the beginning of an interview the interviewee establishes that the interviewer has very little relevant experience of the organisation or context that he or she is apparently studying, and is very naive about the realities of anything outside the academic environment. Having established who is really in control of the interaction, the senior manager may then be prepared to sit back for forty or fifty minutes and respond honestly to the questions of the interviewer. This kind of ritual is of course performed more frequently on young researchers; but even experienced researchers are occasionally caught out by it. Beynon (1988) provides a nice example of a senior NCB manager attacking the credibility of an expert academic witness involved in a colliery inquiry by asking such direct questions as 'Are you qualified to manage a coalfield?', 'What practical management experience have you had in operating?', 'Have you any personal knowledge of selling to commercial buyers?' This form of discrediting the external expert provides a very effective form of corporate defence, and perhaps the minor 'put downs' given to researchers by senior managers may be an anticipatory form of defence just in case the 'wrong' results are produced by the study.

Beynon (1988) also recalls that, when he was interviewing a plant manager, the manager pumped him for information about why a particular group of workers with whom Beynon had also held interviews were proving rather obstructive. Beynon was put in such a position that, if he acceded to this request, he would probably lose the confidence of the workers, but if he directly refused it he would be ejected from the plant by the manager involved. In the event, it appears that he played for time and staged a strategic retreat to the University on account of 'pressing business' until this particular crisis had blown over.

This is, however, an example of what we would call a *macro-political* problem, because the researcher is becoming trapped between two major groups or factions. A similar example occurred when Mark was asked by the works manager of a chemical plant to conduct a study into the consequences of a large plant closure exercise. This exercise had apparently been handled very successfully and had led to the voluntary redundancy of over 1,000 workers, without any overt industrial relations strife. About a week after starting the study Mark noticed that people were starting to become a little less cooperative. Managers seemed to be less available for interview, and people with access to personnel records had suddenly become far too busy to deal with requests. He was, however, very much reassured to be invited to lunch one day with a senior general manager from the site: discussion ranged over the research project which had recently started, and the manager showed much interest in some initial observations. Later the same day he met one of the personnel managers from the site who drew him aside and informed him regretfully that a meeting had been held that same morning to discuss the research project, and that the same general manager with whom he had lunched that day had insisted that the project be stopped.

This was quite a bombshell, because the general manager had not mentioned anything about the meeting, or the decision, at lunch time. What was even more surprising was that the personnel manager seemed to feel that there was nothing exceptional about this behaviour. It subsequently emerged that the decision to ban the project was the focal point in a full scale battle between the works manager and the general manager about the appropriate management style for the site. The former was backing a rather paternalistic line of management, and the results of the study would no doubt have helped him in his argument. His antagonist was arguing for a much harder form of managerialism, and unfortunately for the research project he won the argument. Like many organisational researchers faced with similar problems, Mark was forced to complete the study by interviewing people in their homes, and by using networks of internal contacts provided for another project who would accept some surreptitious questioning about the closure.

The lesson from these political examples is that the researcher needs to be aware of conflicts that may be far deeper and more complex than will be evident to a relative newcomer in the organisation. We can offer three pieces of advice on how to deal with such politics. Firstly, try to identify one or two 'key informants' who may be prepared to help in a disinterested way. They themselves need to be well informed but not directly concerned with the issues under investigation. Informants may be able to advise on who to talk to, and they should be able to explain why things are, or are not, happening. Secondly, deliberately look for people who have different perspectives on key issues. Talk further to them and others in order to understand *why* they hold different views. Thirdly, always assume that there is more than meets the eye. People may withhold information because they believe it is irrelevant, or they may genuinely have forgotten things. In organisations that have a policy of moving people around every two years, the collective memory may be very short. The departmental secretary may be the only person who knows that your topic has already been researched and written up twice in the last five years.

Up to this point we have made no mention of *ethics*. This is because 'ethics' are most frequently discussed in relation to the responsibilities of more powerful people against those who are less powerful. It should be quite evident that, in the examples given above, the researcher is in the less powerful position, the most likely ethical dilemma being whether to betray the confidences given by junior managers, when one is cross-examined by more senior managers. According to Punch (1986), ethical issues frequently arise from a clash between personal and professional interests. In other words, when the researcher for the sake of his or her career wants to obtain some data badly, he or she may overstep the bounds of personal privacy or confidentiality.

Another point worth noting is that most discussions about research ethics concern the use of qualitative methods. This may be simply because qualitative researchers are more sympathetic and sensitive to human feelings and responsibilities. On the other hand, it may be that when using qualitative methods, such as open interviews or participant observation (see Chapter 5), the researcher has far more control about what information is gathered, how it is recorded and how it is interpreted. With quantitative methods it is generally the informant who provides the information directly, by completing questionnaires or whatever, and the researcher simply has to accept what is provided by the informant without having much opportunity to question it. The paradox is that the use of qualitative research methods may put the researcher in a considerably more powerful position in relation to individuals – and hence the additional concern with ethical issues in this case.

Two particular ethical issues frequently concern organisational researchers. The first arises from the use of participant observation research methods which, as Ditton (1977) says, are essentially deceitful. That is, if you are participating in a situation, and at the same time observing and recording (perhaps later) what has taken place, you cannot avoid some deception about your real purposes. For as soon as you explain clearly to those involved precisely what you are doing you cannot continue as a 'normal' participant – unless, of course, you persuade participants to adjust *their* roles so that they become co-researchers. This paradox is structurally woven into the role of the participant observer, and we discuss it further in Chapter 5 in relation to a wider classification of participant/observer roles. The ethical questions for the researcher then concern how much deception in a situation is acceptable, and how far the researcher should go in not betraying the trust of any particular informants.

Our view on this dilemma is that one should only deceive people as far as it is necessary to 'get by'. We agree with Taylor and Bogdan (1984) when they suggest that the researcher, on being asked about the nature and purposes of his work, should, 'Be truthful, but vague and imprecise' (p. 25). This seems to have been the approach adopted by Dalton in his pioneering study of the processes of management. He comments that he was prepared to explain to most of his informants about the nature and purposes of his study, and that in the long run this did not inhibit the majority of his informants (Dalton, 1964).

The second ethical issue is the control and use of data obtained by the researcher. In most cases we can assume that it is the researcher who has this control and ownership, and that therefore she must exercise due ethical responsibility by not publicising or circulating any information that is likely to harm the interests of individual informants, particularly the less powerful ones. There is an interesting story, however, where this particular assumption was neatly turned upon its head. A senior academic was interviewing a member of the British Royal Family, and at the end of the interview he offered to have the tape transcribed and to send a transcript to the interviewee, who would then be asked to strike out any passages to which he objected. The Important Person stretched out a hand, saying, 'No. I shall retain the tape and will let you have the portions that I am prepared to have published.'

But perhaps the most difficult situation arises when the organisation itself is not unduly powerful and the researcher involved is very determined. This clearly happened in the case of Punch's research into the effects on its former pupils of the progressive education provided by Dartington Hall School (Punch, 1986). This resulted in a long drawn out battle over publication rights, where both sides of the debate felt that they had been betrayed by the other side. We shall discuss this example a little further in the final section of the chapter.

Finally, there is an on-going debate about the value, or otherwise, of ethical codes in relation to research. It is argued that at least some codes need to be made explicit in order to ensure that people are alerted to some of the likely ethical dilemmas that they may face. Such codes should also provide some kind of sanction in cases of blatant abuse and exploitation. But there is a problem here. As Snell (1986) points out, ethical issues are extremely complex. They involve not only the dynamics of power but also the competing claims of different ideologies. The danger is that ethical guidelines will not only be too rigid and simplistic to deal with real cases; they will also contain the biases that are inherent in one or another ideological position.

A similar line is taken by Punch (1986), who points out that ethical codes may very easily be constructed to protect the powerful and provide no particular consolation to the weak – who are presumably the people most in need of ethical protection. At the very most he argues that ethical codes should be used as guidelines for practice, rather than as tablets of stone. And, again, Dalton (1964) argues that ethical codes are essentially pluralistic and depend on the viewpoint of the rule-maker: 'The social investigator must sort his values and obligations and weigh them repeatedly throughout the research process. In a democratic society, he cannot impose one fixed code on multiple conflicting codes' (p. 61).

Utilisation of research

The link between research and action is often very weak, and many people find this extremely disappointing. Researchers themselves are only too aware of this feeling when they find that the fruits of several years' labour are gratefully accepted by the sponsoring organisation, whether it be academic or industrial, and are simply filed away in a dust-proof cabinet. Likewise the impact of research on public policy has been rather limited, especially, as Finch (1986) points out, when the methods are essentially qualitative. This is also true in the United States, where the recent AACSB-sponsored survey on management education commented on the widespread dissatisfaction of American companies with the usability of research produced by Business Schools (Porter and McKibbin, 1988).

To some extent this disappointment could simply be a result of different people having different expectations of research. Within the academic world, the expectations are fairly specific. Good research should lead to successful PhDs (completed within target dates), to the publication of articles in refereed journals, and to the timely production of research reports which demonstrate that the work has satisfactorily completed what it set out to do in the first place. Being published in the appropriate academic journals is still very important for the career advancement of academics, and the main political problems are related to debates, cliques and paradigms within the academic world (as we have discussed earlier in this chapter). Fortunately, or not, most academic journals have a very limited circulation outside academia and commercial sponsors are not often concerned about what is likely to be published in these outlets as a result of studies that they have sponsored.

The same cannot be said for publication of books, as Punch (1986) found out to his cost. At the outset of his research with the Dartington Hall Trust he had signed a piece of paper in which he committed himself only to publish with prior permission of the Trust. Initially he regarded this as a mere formality, and therefore he was greatly surprised when the document was used to prevent publication of a book about Dartington Hall School. Given the importance of publications to academic careers, Punch realised that his own career was effectively being blocked by what he regarded as the intransigent position of the organisation he had studied. Conversely Dartington Hall felt that publication of Punch's findings would undoubtedly do harm to the School, and therefore that he should be stopped in his tracks.

The advice of Punch, then, is that the researcher should *never* sign away her rights of publication, and this view is also strongly supported by traditional researchers such as Bulmer (1988). On the other hand, Buchanan et al. (1988) take the more pragmatic line that organisational clients have a right to receive reports from those who research them, and that they should be allowed to comment upon the reports before they are published. This collaborative approach should enable the quality of final reports to be improved, and may also contribute to the maintenance of positive relationships between researchers and clients.

One way of resolving this dilemma is to consider the research 'models' involved. Those adopting the 'military' model will wish to have clear agreements about issues such as access, confidentiality and publication rights agreed well in advance. At the other end of the scale it is very important for the 'investigative journalism' researcher not to sign anything that could be used in evidence against her. This would argue for fudging agreements and avoiding any formal commitments. The two other models, 'private agent' and 'appropriate technology', would represent intermediate cases between these two extremes. If agreements are to be reached in these cases they should ideally specify both the rights that the researcher has to publish, and the right of the client to monitor and control certain kinds of output.

Issues of implementation and utilisation become more serious when one considers the more practical and applied forms of research. When working directly for clients or patrons, as in evaluation research, we have found it very important to tie the research closely to the question that the sponsors or clients want to have answered. This is not a one-off process, but depends on a considerable amount of discussion and negotiation between the needs of the client and the capabilities of the researcher (Easterby-Smith, 1986). Many clients already have a fairly good idea of the likely results from a research study *before* they commission it, and therefore the researcher should pay particular attention to the possibility of disproving what the client thinks to be the case. Success in this respect will lead to the clients learning something new; failure will provide the client with much more confidence in his or her existing beliefs.

The problem of utilisation is not confined to academic research. Innovatory projects conducted within organisations can have just as much difficulty being accepted and implemented. One of the ways that the fast-moving company 3M deals with this problem is to formalise the role of 'sponsor' – usually a senior manager who is prepared to champion a particular idea or project. As Nonaka (1988) comments: 'Before a daring and promising idea can stand on its own, it must be defined and supported by a sponsor willing to risk his or her reputation in order to advance or support changes in intracompany values' (p. 14). Similarly, when in-company research projects have been incorporated into management development programmes it has been found that the close involvement of senior managers as clients is essential if results are to be acted upon (Ashton and Easterby-Smith, 1979).

What remains crucial is the nature and relationship between the researcher and the clients: this needs to be open and honest rather than sycophantic, and above all there should be a reasonable degree of mutual trust. Where the degree of mutual trust is limited we have noticed a marked tendency for clients and sponsors to try to push researchers into more of a 'technician' role, where the researcher is expected to gather data, often quantitative, within a framework defined by the clients. Interpretation of the data is then under the control of the clients rather than the researchers.

To some extent we have assumed above that the responsibility for utilisation and consequent action is the responsibility, and in the capacity, of these clients or patrons. In the case of policy-orientated research it is by no means so simple because one may be dealing with rather complex bureaucracies or political systems. In the case of research geared towards national (social) policy, Finch (1986) points to two distinct traditions and assumptions about the appropriate way of using such research. On the one hand there is the 'social engineering' model, which sees research as a linear and rational process where research studies are commissioned so that their results feed into specific decisions and supply the missing facts to enable decision-makers to take the right course of action. On the other hand there is the 'enlightenment' model, which sees implementation as an incremental process with lots of diffuse viewpoints being introduced from different levels of the social system, hence providing an *indirect* link between the research and policy implications. The former model makes full use of quantitative methods, and the latter has a preference for qualitative methods.

As one might expect, most governments and sponsoring agencies prefer to use the social engineering kind of research because it gives them more power and control over what will take place. But the problem with the largely quantitative studies implied by this model is that they can only describe the situation as it is now, or as it was in the past; they can give very little guidance on what should take place in the future, and this is a limitation when research is supposed to be aiding policy formulation. This is where the more democratic enlightenment model can help to some extent by providing a much wider range of options and ideas in order to guide future action.

But it still remains unpopular amongst sponsors, and attracts criticism from some academic quarters. Gubrium and Silverman (1989), for example, argue that even when the enlightenment model is used to provide knowledge of alternative possibilities and problems to administrators, it is still acting largely in the interests of 'the establishment'. The simple idea that the fruits of the social sciences will lead to improvements of the human condition serves as a justification for the distinction between those who make, and those who are affected by, the rules of society. This disguises the reality of power by suggesting that it is the property of one or other group in society – rather than it being implicit in all relationships, like capillaries in the social body.

So what are the implications for the researcher? Firstly it is important to recognise that power and political issues will be significant even when, or perhaps especially when, they are not obviously present. Secondly, there are no easy answers, or solutions, to the political web. It exists in the form of ideologies, of personal interests (including those of the researchers), of power differences and of ethical dilemmas.

This suggests that the researcher needs both clarity of purpose, and much flexibility in tackling problems. Much clarity of purpose can come from awareness, both of one's own interests, and of one's assumptions about the world and how best to investigate it. We have discussed these issues in the last two chapters. In the next part of the book we turn to consider the range of methods and techniques that are at the disposal of the researcher. We stress consistently that these should not be seen as entirely free-standing, but should be subordinated to the considerations of purpose and philosophy that have been outlined above.

PART THREE
Doing and Completing the Research

5
Qualitative Methods

The three chapters in this part of the book considers ways of gathering data, making sense of it, and completing the research process. Chapters 5 and 6 respectively look at the use of qualitative and quantitative methods for data collection and analysis, and the final chapter looks at the problems of writing up, and capitalising on, research results.

In this chapter we consider techniques primarily associated with qualitative methods: interviews, observation and diary methods. Questionnaires and survey methods are tackled in the following chapter, not because they are always quantitative methods, but because they are easily used in a quantitative way, and they therefore provide a framework around which to discuss issues of quantitative methods.

Many of the qualitative methods discussed here are simply devices whereby the researcher, once close to organisational members, can gain the sort of insights into people and situations she requires. Others are useful as aids or tools to help the respondents think about their own worlds and consider, possibly for the first time, the way they construct their reality.

Van Maanen (1983) defines qualitative methods as 'an array of interpretive techniques which seek to describe, decode, translate and otherwise come to terms with the meaning, not the frequency, of certain more or less naturally occurring phenomena in the social world' (p. 9).

The most fundamental of all qualitative methods is that of in-depth interviewing, and for this reason we have examined its use in detail. But there are a range of lesser known 'instruments' that provide useful ways of supplementing interviews and help to probe for insights into how respondents see their world. We have chosen to present six of these 'instruments' or approaches and have briefly discussed the use of each, pointing to further literature where appropriate. These are – critical incident technique, repertory grid technique, projective techniques, protocol analysis, group interviews and cognitive mapping. As mentioned, the other chief qualitative methods are observation and diary methods, which we have also covered here.

The latter part of the chapter examines the different ways in which qualitative data can be managed and analysed, and the circumstances under which each method is most appropriate.

Interviewing

Before adopting any method of data collection, the objectives for the research need to be clearly decided. Choosing to interview is no exception to this, as interviews can be highly formalised and structured (for example those used in market research), or they can be akin to a free-ranging conversation.

Although interviewing is often claimed to be 'the best' method of gathering information, its complexity can sometimes be underestimated. It is time consuming to undertake interviews properly, and they are sometimes used when other methods might be more appropriate. If researchers wish to obtain answers to a number of fairly simple questions then a questionnaire might well be more appropriate. Face-to-face interviewing in this case might only provide the researcher with access to the individuals who will answer the questions. These highly structured interviews would be based on a carefully prepared set of questions piloted and refined until the researcher is convinced of their 'validity'. The assumption is made that the interviewer will ask each interviewee the same question in the same tone of voice. The simplest form of such interviews are those where there are short answers to questions and the interviewer simply ticks boxes and no deep thought is required by either party. These are the type of interviews that take place in the shopping precincts of most towns and cities every Saturday morning. The primary aim of such 'interviewing' is to gain a 'quantitative' result: 20% of the sample said this and 10% said that. Large numbers (hundreds and thousands) are required in order to provide confidence that the responses obtained can be generalised to the population at large.

As with most types of research, there are some compromise positions. A positivistic approach can be retained where the interview follows a fairly standardised set of questions, whilst offering some flexibility, and allowing the views of the interviewee to become known. This type of interview might be appropriate, for example, when questions require a good deal of thought and when responses need to be explored and clarified. This process often gives an added degree of confidence to the replies which are not available in questionnaires. In addition, the interviewer does have the opportunity to identify non-verbal clues which are present, for example, in the inflection of the voice, facial expressions or the clothes that the interviewee is wearing, and these can be used to develop secondary questions. Although this type of research is conducted by interview, the standards by which it is judged are those that apply to quantitative questionnaires, and readers should refer to Chapter 6 when considering their use.

The present section deals primarily with interviews where the primary purpose of the interview is to understand the meanings interviewees attach to issues and situations in contexts that are not structured in advance by the researcher's assumptions.

This method of data collection was much used by Rosemary Stewart in her research on the nature of managerial work. The importance of interviews is summarised by Burgess (1982): '(the interview) is . . . the opportunity for the researcher to probe deeply to uncover new clues, open up new dimensions of a problem and to secure vivid, accurate inclusive accounts that are based on personal experience' (p. 107). Most interviews are conducted on a one-to-one basis, between the interviewer and the interviewee.

The label 'qualitative interview' has been used to describe a broad range of different types of interview, from those that are supposedly totally 'non-directive' or 'open' to those where the interviewer takes to the interview a prepared list of questions which he or she is determined to ask, come what may '. . . between these two extremes is an abyss of practice and therefore theory about the purpose and nature of the qualitative interview' (p. 45). As she describes, the main reason for conducting qualitative interviews is to understand . . . 'how individuals construct the meaning and significance of their situations . . . from . . . the complex personal framework of beliefs and values, which they have developed over their lives in order to help explain and predict events in their world'. Researchers must therefore be able to conduct interviews so that the opportunity is present for these insights to be gained. Failure to achieve this might well result in a superficial exchange of information, which might well have been better and more cost effectively achieved via a semi-structured questionnaire.

In order to be able to achieve these insights the researcher will need to be sensitive enough, and skilled enough, to ensure that she not only understands the other person's views but also, at times, assists individuals to explore their own beliefs. Later in this chapter we will discuss a number of techniques that might help the researcher do this to advantage.

Interviews, semi-structured or unstructured, are therefore appropriate methods when:

(a) it is necessary to understand the constructs that the interviewee uses as a basis for her opinions and beliefs about a particular matter or situation;
(b) one aim of the interview is to develop an understanding of the respondent's 'world' so that the researcher might influence it, either independently or collaboratively as might be the case with action research.

In addition they are useful when:

(a) the step-by-step logic of a situation is not clear;
(b) the subject matter is highly confidential or commercially sensitive;
(c) the interviewee may be reluctant to be truthful about this issue other than confidentially in a one-to-one situation.

The degree of structure

Jones (1985) highlights a number of issues that researchers will need to consider in order for interviews to be successful. The first is the problem which all researchers must resolve – how much structure to put in the interview. She makes the point that:

> . . . there is no such thing as presuppositionless research. In preparing for interviews researchers will have, and should have, some broad questions in mind, and the more interviews they do and the more patterns they see in the data, the more likely they are to use this grounded understanding to want to explore in certain directions rather than others. (p. 47)

In a study conducted by Richard, employees and managers were interviewed together. By mixing the interviews he was not only able to compare the way the different people viewed situations, but it enabled better lines of inquiry to be developed and provided the opportunity to check out emergent themes and patterns as the interviews progressed. On a purely practical note, as these interviews all took place within two days, Richard remembers being quite saturated with information, and a consideration might have been to spread them out over a longer period.

Researchers, then, are free and encouraged to make choices as they collect their data as to which line of questioning they should explore further and which lines of inquiry to discard. They do need a framework from which to begin to plot out the developing themes but, as Jones reminds us, although researchers are to some extent tied to their frameworks they shouldn't be 'tied up by them'. One way in which this can be achieved is to prepare a 'topic guide' which can be used as a loose structure for the questions. Although there may be some deviation from the sequence so as to follow interesting lines of inquiry and to facilitate an unbroken discussion, the interviewer should attempt to cover all the issues mentioned.

Finally, on the subject of structure, the researcher should be warned against assuming that a 'non-directive' interview, where the interviewee talks freely without interruption or intervention, is the way to achieve a clear picture of the interviewee's perspective. This is far from true. It is more likely to produce no clear picture in the mind of the interviewee of what questions or issues the interviewer is interested in, and in the mind of the interviewer of what questions the interviewee is answering! Too many assumptions of this kind lead to poor data which is difficult to interpret. Researchers are therefore likely to be more successful if they are clear at the outset about the exact areas of their interest.

Interviewing skills
Understanding issues from an interviewee's point of view can be extremely difficult, especially when the respondent himself may not have a clearly articulated view of the answers to the questions posed, or may not wish to divulge sensitive information. It is here that the skills of the interviewer come to the fore.

McClelland (1965) has conducted careful studies about common sense notions concerning motivations. He claims that people cannot be trusted to say exactly what their motives are, as they often get ideas about their own motives from commonly accepted half-truths. For example, a person may say that he is interested in achievement because he has made money. But a careful check using different probing methods may reveal quite a different picture. Often people simply aren't aware of their own motives. Mangham (1986) met this problem in his studies of managerial competence. He found that although many managers complained that they needed subordinates who could better motivate staff, when they were asked what exactly they meant by motivation they gave ambiguous answers and became confused.

From a 'positivistic' standpoint, the fact that there is a contradiction as to the meaning of 'motivation' invalidates the research. But for the in-depth interviewer who probes, questions and checks, this is important data. The fact that people are confused and can't agree on what they mean by motivation or the way they construct particular situations is the essence of the research and is the learning that is acquired.

The skills of an interviewer centre around the ability to recognise what is relevant and remember it, or tape it, so that afterwards detailed notes can be made. This requires the interviewer to be perceptive and sensitive to events, so that lines of inquiry can be changed and adapted during the interview. Above all, interviewers need to be able to listen, and to refrain from projecting their own opinions or feelings into the situation. This is more difficult than it sounds, since one of the ways of obtaining trust is to empathise with the respondent. The interviewer needs to listen to what interviewees want to say, and what they do not want to say, without helping them (Mayo, 1949). Non-verbal data might be crucial in providing clues to these situations, for example the loss of eye contact, or a changed facial expression.

From time to time as patterns or uncertainties arise from the interview, it is useful to check one's understanding by summarising what has been said. This should be presented as a way of seeking clarification. The process of 'testing out' is a way of safeguarding against assuming too quickly that understanding has been achieved.

Social interaction
The interviewer needs also to understand the importance placed on the social interaction between interviewer and interviewee. Jones (1985) suggests people will attribute meaning and significance to the particular research situations they are in. The questions an interviewer may ask and the answers an interviewee gives will often depend on the way in which their situations are defined.

From the point of view of the interviewer, certain conclusions may be drawn from the dress, mannerisms, voice or language of the interviewee which can in part formulate the attitude taken to that person. Wrong assumptions made from non-verbals might also bias attitudes in other ways. Richard recalls one interview when the union convenor wore a sports jacket, in complete contrast to the other men who wore overalls and boots. This raised questions in his mind about the convener's relationship with both men and management.

Similarly Jones (1985) points out that interviewees will 'suss out' what researchers are like, and make judgements from their first impressions about whether the interviewer can be trusted or whether they might be 'damaged' in some way by data that could be so used. Such suspicions do not necessarily mean that interviewees will refuse to be interviewed, but it might mean, as Jones indicates, that they just: '. . . seek to get the interview over as quickly as possible, with enough detail and enough feigned interest to satisfy the researcher that he or she is getting something of value but without saying anything that touches the core of what is actually believed and cared about in the research' (p. 50).

Clearly, therefore, social interaction is an important factor in qualitative interviewing, and an important ingredient in all the methods we discuss is trust.

Obtaining trust

Trust is an important and difficult issue in interviews, especially in one-off interviews where the people involved have not met before. Failure to develop trust may well result in interviewees simply resorting to telling the researcher what they think the researcher wants to know. But an open and trusting relationship may not be possible or sufficient when dealing with particular elites or individuals in positions of power as we have discussed in Chapter 4. It often helps if the researcher is viewed as having equal status to the manager, and also if the manager feels he might gain from the exchange. There are some practical ways to achieve this.

The first point is to ensure that you are well clued up about the company. By tracking down a couple of annual reports and recruitment literature in advance you should be able to appear 'on the ball'. When making initial contact our experience suggests that a phone call is often better than a letter; but be prepared to make two or three calls before the right contact is established. Contrary to common belief, managers are surprisingly ready to talk over the telephone and the 'voice' contact is a first opportunity to communicate enthusiasm for the project. Take full advantage of the opportunity, but be aware that at the same time the manager will be weighing up the likely costs (and benefits) of the potential intrusion.

When talking about research it is important to use appropriate language. It is not a good strategy to unnerve the possible gatekeeper by using too many theoretical concepts. Here are a few examples of the way words may be interpreted:

Student: implies an unskilled 'amateurish' inquiry, which may be unthreatening.

Researcher: implies that there might be a more professional relationship, but that questions of access might need to be managed carefully.

Interview: gives the impression of a formal structured interrogation which is controlled by the researcher.

Discussion: may make the manager feel more relaxed and less threatened, with the potential for genuine exchange.

Survey: is often understood to be the kind of study where findings are aggregated too much to be of use.

Preliminary telephone calls are best followed up by letter. This fulfils three purposes. One is credibility, especially if the letter is on the notepaper of an independent body – a university, polytechnic or college. Secondly, it may assist cooperation in the future; and thirdly, it provides the opportunity to send further details about the research. This is the opportunity to set out in detail what is required.

A further piece of advice is to avoid being over-anxious about getting all the data in one go. Relationships take time to form. It may be better to undertake a series of short interviews from which a useful dialogue flows, rather than to act hastily and alienate the interviewees through lots of pushy questioning.

The location of the interview and the setting in which it takes place can also be important. Richard found in one project that adverse results were produced by conducting interviews in the manager's office because the employees being interviewed were uncertain as to the confidentiality of what they might say. Interviewing on 'neutral territory', for example in a car or in the works canteen, might have alleviated the problem.

One strategy used by a colleague of ours, which worked to his advantage, was to interview well away from the workplace. When researching into aspects of management development, he undertook his fieldwork by sitting in the first class compartments of British Rail trains. He would sit next to executive-looking individuals, armed only with a folder marked Management Development, in the hope that managers would talk to him. This they usually did, and without prompts he was able to elicit their views on a range of management development issues. What struck Neil was the extent to which the views and opinions expressed by managers, off guard and to a person they were unlikely ever to meet again, contradicted the 'reality' contained in much contemporary management literature. Had the interview take place in the manager's office, the results might well have been quite different.

This example not only illustrates how a researcher managed to obtain data that the manager might have found hard to articulate in his office; it also shows how a method can be undertaken in a 'natural setting' where each views the other as having equal status. This kind of research would normally be extremely costly, yet it does illustrate the lengths that might be required to obtain data.

In another example, in which we have been involved – that of researching small business owners – we have found that relationships have often developed quickest when interviewees are first engaged in general discussions about their business. This is something which they know and understand. Whatever focus subsequent questions have, answers have context that is useful and are answered with much less informality.

Finally, there is the question of the effects of using audio tape recording in interviews. The decision on whether or not to use a tape recorder depends much on an interviewee's anxiety about confidentiality and the use to which any information divulged can be put.

There are ways in which anxiety can be minimised, for example, by handing over the responsibility for switching the tape on and off to the interviewee, so that when she does not wish certain parts of the interview to be recorded, she can just switch off the machine. But although using a tape recorder aids the listening process and gives the opportunity of an unbiased record of a interviewee's responses, it is in our view counterproductive to lose potentially revealing insights by its use. Most managers are not self-conscious when interviews are recorded and quickly forget the machine; but for others notes may be the only answer. The deciding factor should not be whether or not to tape, or whether permission will or will not be given, but rather what effect its use will have on the interview interaction in terms of the relationship and the data created.

Interview bias
Readers will see in the next chapter, on quantitative research, that minimal interview bias – the consistency with which questions are put and the lack of ambiguity in their meaning – is regarded as crucial. In in-depth interviewing the issue is slightly different. As views and questioning approaches will differ from one interview to the next, there is no one 'objective' view to be discovered which the process of interviewing may 'bias'. However, there is a very real concern about interviewers imposing their own reference frame on the interviewees, both when the questions are asked and as the answers are interpreted.

The researcher is in something of a dilemma for, as has been suggested in an earlier section, open questions may avoid bias, but they are not always the best way of obtaining the desired information, nor are they always the best way of putting an interviewee at ease. But the issue of bias gives a pull in the other direction. In order to avoid bias, there is often the tendency for researchers to leave questions 'open'. There will be some occasions when researchers will want to focus on discovering responses to specific alternatives, and in this case 'probes' can be useful as an intervention technique to improve, or sharpen up, the interviewee's response.

There are a number of alternative ways in which these can be used:

1 The *basic probe* simply involves repeating the initial question and is useful when the interviewee seems to be wandering off the point.
2 *Explanatory probes* involve building onto incomplete or vague statements made by the respondent. Ask questions such as: 'What did you mean by that?', 'What makes you say that?'
3 *Focused probes* are used to obtain specific information. Typically one would ask the respondent 'What sort of . . .?'
4 The *silent probe* is one of the most effective techniques to use when the respondent is either reluctant or very slow to answer the question posed. Simply pause and let her break the silence.
5 The technique of *drawing out* can be used when the interviewee has halted, or dried up. Repeat the last few words she said, and then look expectant or say, 'Tell me more about that', 'What happened then?'
6 *Giving ideas or suggestions* involves offering the interviewee an idea to think about – 'Have you thought about . . .?' 'Have you tried . . .?' 'Did you know that . . .?' 'Perhaps you should ask Y. . .'
7 *Mirroring or reflecting* involves expressing in your own words what the respondent has just said. This is very effective because it may force the respondent to rethink her answer and construct another reply which will amplify the previous answer – 'What you seem to be saying/feeling is . . .'

To avoid bias, probes should never lead. An example of a leading probe, might be: 'So you would say that you were really satisfied?' Instead the interviewer should say: 'Can you explain a little more?' or 'How do you mean?'

Relevance to interviewees

The relevance of the research to interviewees is another factor that will affect the quality of the data provided. Maruyama (1981) has explored the attitudes of prison inmates to researchers such as sociologists or newspaper reporters. Because they regard them as exploiting their situation for reasons such as an enhanced reputation and career advancement they tend to invent plausible but untrue responses in order to minimise the intrusion such research often represents. There are some salutary lessons here for many researchers in management.

But not all interaction or questioning produces answers that are threatening or potentially damaging, particularly in management. On the contrary, many individuals find benefit in talking to an independent outsider about themselves or learning something about future changes in the organisation as in action research. Researchers should be able to recognise and capitalise on these situations and offer them as benefits or advantages to interviewees in exchange for participation. The more willing they are to be open the more they are likely to gain.

In addition, interest and commitment shown by the interviewer often produces far better results than clinical detachment. There are several practical ways in which this can be achieved. One way is by conducting more than one interview, or by offering the interviewee the opportunity to comment on the transcripts of the tape or on written-up field notes. Another is to offer interviewees a summary of the results or conclusions, and to make sure that one is sent to them. These strategies are not just 'ploys' to obtain compliance with a researcher's wishes; they can, for example, form important ways of validating data and gaining new insights.

In some kinds of research there can be more immediate benefits to participation. In action research, for example, where change is one objective of the research, the researcher's role can be viewed as a cross between an 'importer' of new knowledge to organisational members and a medium through which individuals can express the way they view the organisation or change. By working on the change process and by operating in this way, researchers and the organisation will often gain the kind of contextual information, behavioural as well as structural, that can assist the change process, as well as enabling the participants in the research to gain a better understanding of their organisation and their role within it. This is particularly important at times of change, as individuals have a natural concern about how change might affect them.

In other forms of action research, for example in the group interviewing technique called 'cognitive mapping' which we discuss later, change is seen as a primary objective, and information is shared between the organisational members. In this technique the researcher can facilitate exploration of organisation members' perceptions, views and beliefs in relation to particular organisational problems. Through such processes interviewees become involved in activities which are both meaningful and useful to them.

Ethics and choices

In Chapter 4 we reviewed some of the main ethical issues that may be encountered in any forms of management research. These are particularly pertinent in the case of 'interviewing' because of the potential freedom within the interaction for exchanging information and interpretations. It is for this reason that organisations may be hostile to totally open interviews, and it is not unusual for researchers to be asked for a copy of the interview schedule before access is granted. In this way the organisation, or factions within it, may feel the potential risk involved is reduced.

The ethical issues relating to individual respondents concern the 'micro-politics' of the organisation. Despite assurances given about confidentiality (which normally mean not revealing *raw* data to anyone else in the same organisation), it is virtually impossible to hide everything that has been said. In qualitative interviews the focus will inevitably be affected by data and impressions obtained from earlier interviews. As we noted in Chapter 4, it is not beyond the wit of managers to infer from the questions asked what kind of information has already been obtained by the interviewer, and from whom. Thus it is important for the interviewer to be aware of the possible interests of the interviewee, and how these could be harmed by indirect disclosures of the wrong information.

The same point applies to the style or degree of intervention that researchers should make overall, and many ideal situations will be tempered by such things as resource availability and the ease of access. However, much of what will be possible will depend upon the nature of the relationship that develops, and whether sufficient trust has been formed.

What is important is that researchers understand these issues when dealing with interviews. By understanding the implications of the choices they make they will be better placed to recognise any effect they may have on the nature of the relationship formed, and therefore on the data that is collected. Hirschman (1986) gives some useful and practical insights into the ethical issues when collecting, interpreting and presenting results.

Ways of supplementing interviews

Critical incident technique

One method of teasing out information which might not be readily expressed is proposed by Flanagan (1957). He called it critical incident technique. Flanagan defines it as 'a set of procedures for collecting direct observations of human behaviour in such a way as to facilitate their potential usefulness in solving practical problems and developing broad psychological principles'. By 'incident' Flanagan meant any observable human activity that is sufficiently complete in itself to permit inference or prediction to be made about the person performing the act. To be 'critical' the incident must occur in a situation where the purpose or intent of the act seems fairly clear to the observer and when its consequences are sufficiently definite to leave little doubt concerning its effect.

The classic example often quoted to illustrate the technique was the way in which the American army investigated the large number of helicopter crashes that were occurring particularly when landing in groups. By concentrating their research only on what the pilot recalled of the 'critical incident' when control of the aircraft was lost they were able to build up a picture of the particular circumstances when most crashes happened. It was found that control was lost at the moment of landing but the 'critical incident' was the moment when the pilot viewed the ground through another helicopter's rotor blades.

In his writings, Flanagan describes his technique from a highly 'objectivist' standpoint, claiming its value as being able to bridge the gap between the observation and the recording and interpretation of the reasons behind actions. But the technique has also been used by qualitative researchers to great effect, particularly in conjunction with in-depth interviews. Respondents might, for example, be asked to track back to particular instances in their work lives and to explain their actions and motives with specific regard to those instances. In Richard's research he has used the technique to ask owner/managers of small companies what had been their particular barriers to growth. At a given point in the interview he would ask if there had been any particular problems in the development of the company. He would then encourage the manager to explain that problem in some detail and illustrate how the problem was eventually surmounted. From this example he would begin to develop ideas about how individuals managed particular problems and about the information they used in doing this. It is important to use material that can be substantiated since there are criticisms of the technique relating to recall, and the natural tendency of individuals to use hindsight in rationalising the past. One technique which overcomes this problem is protocol analysis, and we shall discuss it later.

MacKinlay (1986), when undertaking research into a housing authority, used the critical incident technique in a most unusual way. His 'open' questionnaire was targeted directly at house-holders; it was intentionally made simple, the number of questions being set at only six to enable easy completion. The phrases used in the questions were clear, without any extensive technical or ambiguous wording. Each question allowed a third of an A4 page for a reply, but some respondents added additional sheets. The questions concentrated on the primary area of interest and were preceded by the brief explanation: 'These questions are open-ended and I have kept them to a few vital areas of interest. All will require you to reflect back on decisions and reasons for decisions you have made.'

The questions themselves were short and to the point:

1 Please think about an occasion you improved your home. What improvements did you make?
2 On that occasion what made you do it?
3 Did you receive any help? If 'yes', please explain what help you received.
4 Have you wanted to improve your home in any other way but could not?
5 What improvements did you wish to make?
6 What stopped you from doing it?

Data analysis was carried out using a grounded theory approach, which will be discussed later in the chapter.

Repertory grid technique

Another useful technique for investigating areas that are hard to articulate is the repertory grid. The technique is used to understand individuals' perceptions and the constructs they use to understand and manage their world. A repertory grid is a mathematical representation of an individual's perceptions that helps to focus analysis and makes it easier to communicate these perceptions to others. Repertory grids can also be used with people who have low verbal ability, making them particularly useful for children and people with language difficulties. A student of Richard's, piloting the repertory grid technique for his research, used it on his children to find out what they wanted for Christmas. The technique has a strong track record and has been used extensively in areas such as career guidance or job specifications.

The repertory grid is based on the Personal Construct Theory of George Kelly (1955), who regarded individuals as 'scientists' in their own right, continually exploring and developing understanding of their worlds. In doing this they develop cognitive maps for all significant aspects of their experience – which then define, and limit, their potential repertories of behaviour. It follows from such a theory that if we can find ways of drawing a personal map then we are in a position either to understand behaviour, or possibly to alter the map and change behaviour. A repertory grid is a tool for uncovering an individual's view of his world and it contains the following features:

1 *Elements*: or the objects of thought. These objects are usually the other people in the world about us, but they can be inanimate objects or abstract ideas such as, for example, the individual's view of the skills she possesses and how these skills were learnt.
2 *Constructs*: These are the 'qualities' which the individual uses to describe and differentiate between the elements. These are the spectacles with which she views the world outside.
3 *Linking mechanisms*: There are various ways of indicating how the elements and constructs are linked, and of presenting them in matrix form.

The standard procedure for generating a repertory grid is as follows: firstly, decide on the *focus* of the grid. This should be quite specific and the interviewee should be reminded of it at regular intervals. These might be the qualities required of a manager in a particular function, the particular work content of a given job, or the features of products currently competing with one's own.

Secondly, select with the interviewee a group of elements (between 5 and 10) which are relevant to the chosen focus, and which are also likely to provide a good range. If, for example, the focus of the grid was on the skills required of a manager it would be appropriate to choose individuals who were familiar to the interviewee, some of whom he regarded as particularly able, some of average ability, and some of below-average ability.

Thirdly, constructs are elicited, usually by asking the respondent to compare and contrast elements in groups of three, known as triads. Each element is written on a card and then three cards are selected at random. The interviewee is asked to decide which pair of cards are similar in a way which also makes them distinct from the third. He or she is asked to provide a word or phrase which describes the pairs, and a contrasting word or phrase to describe the remaining card. For example, in the case of a grid with the focus on competences required of a manager, someone might choose two cards of named people as similar because they see them both as *dynamic*, and the third as *staid*. In this case the construct elicited is a continuum on which *dynamic* is at one end and *staid* is at the other. This process is repeated with different triads of elements until a reasonable number of constructs (perhaps 6 to 10) have been produced.

Fourthly, each of the elements needs to be linked to, or rated against, each of the constructs. This can be done several different ways: by deciding which of the two 'poles' of the construct provides the best description of the element; by determining the position of the element on a rating scale (often 7 points) constructed between the poles of each construct; or by rank-ordering each of the elements along the dimension indicated by each of the constructs. The results of these ratings or rankings are recorded as ticks and crosses, or as numbers in a matrix.

Figure 5.1 shows a grid that was completed by a training officer prior to attending a trainer development programme. It was intended to explore both his view of his current role, and his expectations of the programme he was about to attend.

Small grids can be analysed manually, or by eye, by looking for patterns of relationships and differences between constructs and elements. This can form the basis of an interesting collaborative discussion between interviewer and interviewee. With larger grids (say, 5 × 5, or upwards) it is more common to use computer analysis packages. There are two main families of these, based either on principal components analysis, or on cluster analysis. The former produces a map which plots the elements within dimensions, and axes, defined by the constructs (see Figure 5.2 for a mappling of the grid in Figure 5.1). The latter produces a kind of 'tree' diagram (dendrogram) which shows how the elements link to each other and how the constructs link to each other.

Although not derived by the repertory grid technique, Figure 5.3 shows a good example of a dendrogram. This example from Hofstede's research (1983) shows the similarities and differences in cross-cultural values in 53 countries and regions of the world. The values used to produce this were drawn from the power distance, uncertainty avoidance, individualism and masculinity indices described in Chapter 3.

The dendrogram should be read from right to left and splits firstly into two large clusters which comprise Ghana through to Jamaica and from Austria through to Finland. The next lower clusters comprise Austria through to South Africa and Denmark through to Finland, and so on down to the greatest degrees of similarity on the far left of the dendrogram.

Advantages and disadvantages of this approach are set out by Stewart and Stewart (1981). The main advantages are that:

1 it involves verbalising constructs which otherwise would remain hidden;
2 it is based on the individual's own framework, not that of the expert; and
3 it provides insights for both the researcher and the researched.

The main disadvantages are that:

1 grids are very hard work to complete and can take considerable periods of time: a 20 × 10 matrix can take up to one and a half hours to complete;
2 grids require a degree of skill from the interviewer if the interviewee's construct framework is to be fully explored;
3 grids may be difficult to analyse and interpret, and there is some danger that people will rely on the structure of the technique to produce packaged, rather than meaningful results;
4 the technique has become 'popular' and as a consequence is sometimes used mechanistically while forgetting the underlying theory of personal constructs.

For those interested in learning more about the repertory grid technique, it has been well written up in a number of publications. For example, Bannister and Fransella (1971) provide a classic overview of the theory and method; Stewart and Stewart (1981) review business applications; and Easterby-Smith (1980) illustrates a number of applications in the field of human resource development.

Projective techniques
The rationale for these techniques is that individuals will reveal hidden levels of their consciousness by reacting to different types of stimuli, such as drawings. These stimuli are intended to be very ambiguous in the hope that the respondents will 'project' their own meaning and significance onto the drawings. In so doing they declare aspects of their innermost motives and feelings which can be interpreted by trained psychologists.

Psychologists such as Freud (see Hall, 1954) and Rogers (1967) claim that there are at least three important barriers which provide blockages to the discovery of an individual's innermost motives. These are:

1 repression and the unconscious

Constructs			(1) Myself as I am	(2) Training Officer in ITB	(3) A progressive manager	(4) A conservative manager	(5) An effective trainer	(6) A less-than-effective trainer	(7) Myself expected at end of course	(8) Me when I took this job	
A	practical	1–7	5	5	4	3	4	4	3	5	academic
B	sensitive	1–7	2	5	3	1	3	6	2	3	insensitive
C	self-motivated	1–7	5	3	2	6	2	1	2	4	not very self-motivated
D	extrovert	1–7	4	2	3	6	2	1	2	5	introvert
E	committed to companies	1–7	1	5	1	1	2	6	1	1	committed to ITB
F	worked hard	1–7	3	2	1	5	2	2	1	3	not needed to work hard

Figure 5.1 *Pre-course grid for Group Training Officer (GTO)*

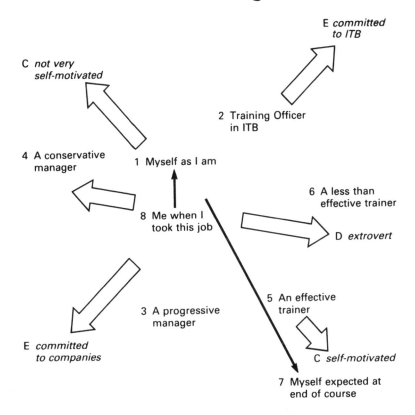

E *committed*
to ITB

C *not very*
self-motivated

2 Training Officer
in ITB

4 A conservative
manager

1 Myself as I am

6 A less than
effective trainer

8 Me when I
took this job

D *extrovert*

5 An effective
trainer

3 A progressive
manager

E *committed*
to companies

C *self-motivated*

7 Myself expected at
end of course

Figure 5.2 *Mapping of elements with space defined by three*
key constructs. (Open arrows indicate dimensions, solid arrows
indicate directions of personal movements)

2 self-awareness and rationality
3 social influences.

Personally we see the value of projective techniques as being confined to specific applications, since they always require 'expert analysis'. In many quarters they are also viewed with scepticism and suspicion. Projective techniques are useful exploratory devices which can reveal hidden aspects of personality or begin a dialogue between researcher and those researched. The technique is widely used in market research (Jobber and Horgan, 1987) in the attempt to establish deep-seated feelings about such things as: the basic motivation to buy or not to buy, consumer reaction to colours, size and shape of packaging, or names of products.

A common form of projective test is the thematic apperception

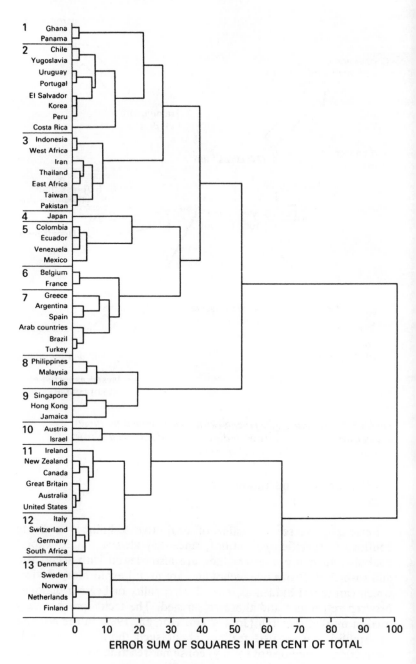

Figure 5.3 *Cluster analysis dendrogram of cross cultural values in 53 countries and regions. Hofstede (1983)*

test (TAT) which asks individuals simply to write a story; the researcher's task is then to find themes in what people say. One way of prompting stories is by the use of photographs. The technique was first used by Henry Murray (1938) and has been developed by David McClelland (1961) as a means of measuring the strength of an individual's need for achievement. McClelland found that a distinctive achievement motive could be isolated and stimulated. The strength of the motive could be measured by taking samples of a person's spontaneous thoughts, such as making up a story about a picture which had been shown, then counting the frequency of mentions about doing things better. Although the procedure involves quite a lot of subjective judgement, researchers who have been trained in the procedure can reach a high degree of consistency in scoring stories.

Whereas the critical incident technique deals with past behaviour, projective tests focus on present behaviour, and this is often of more interest to management researchers as a predictor of future behaviour. For example, the approach has been used in the selection of public house managers for a large brewery chain. In the test to select pub managers a question is posed such as: 'Suppose somebody comes into your pub you know well as a good and valued customer. He says, "Lend me £20 because I've got a certainty for a horse running in the 3.30." What would you do?'

The candidate is asked to explain, or 'project', what he would do in that situation. The more desirable answers will indicate that the individual is sensible enough to decline in such a way that the customer is retained along with the goodwill. The scanning for themes is very similar to employing a grounded approach to data analysis and content analysis, both of which will be described later in the section.

The technique is used extensively in recruitment, and many consulting companies, particularly in the USA, offer a profiling service to aid recruitment and selection of staff.

Protocol analysis

Protocol analysis provides another way of finding out the underlying logic of the way people think and as such fits within the social constructionist perspective. It has been used successfully in the area of market research where researchers are trying to uncover the elements and stages (protocols) in the buying decision. Because the considerations and values held by consumers are uncovered, product mapping is possible and buying behaviour becomes better understood.

Protocol analysis seeks explanations as soon as possible after the event has occurred, and is therefore less affected than techniques such as critical incident by the tendency to rationalise and re-evaluate past experience.

Episodes or protocols unique to an individual, for example during a decision-making situation, form the focus of analysis, and the person is asked to comment on what is going on, either as it happens or, when that is difficult, from a tape recording of the incident. The 'analysis' refers both to the fact that the individual may be analysing events in his life, and that the researchers may analyse the taped discussions for themes that are relevant to their research.

Protocol analysis was used in research undertaken by Burgoyne and Hodgson (1983) which had the objective of describing and understanding managerial action and how managers learned. The method they adopted was as follows:

1 A general context interview was held to explore areas such as the manager's work, activities, role and use of time.
2 Actual incidents from her work life were observed and recorded, and where possible she was asked to think aloud during the incident.
3 Shortly after recording the real-time incident, the manager was asked to recall thoughts and feelings during the incident and to describe why she felt, acted or responded in the way she did.
4 Another meeting was held with her some weeks or months later about:
   (a) further developments in the stream of events of which the episodes were a part;
   (b) consequences of action taken, choice made or orientations adopted during the episodes;
   (c) her current interpretation of phenomena, process and relationships pertinent to the incident.

Protocol analysis, in common with many techniques we have discussed so far, aims to get managers to talk. Of course, as we have acknowledged earlier, individuals might well censor their thoughts before articulation and the method may have limitations in understanding aspects that might be unconscious, semi-conscious, or simply of a non-verbal form. However, the immediacy of the process is a check against too much retrospection and the technique, providing trust can be developed, appears to facilitate open statements and descriptions. Burgoyne and Hodgson comment that the very act of discussing incidents or protocols with individuals actually facilitates the development of trust, so that in their study people found it much easier later on to explain what had been going on in their minds. Burgoyne and Hodgson cite two other methodological issues that arise out of such an approach. These are common to all in-depth approaches: (i) the nature of the researcher/respondent relationship, which we have already discussed in the section on interviewing; and (ii) the general problem of analysing experiential and descriptive data. Since this is a general problem in qualitative research it will be discussed in a later section.

Group interviews

Interviews need not necessarily take place on a one-to-one basis, and for some types of investigation group interviews can be very useful. These take the form of loosely structured 'steered conversations'. They are used extensively in market research, where they are known as 'focus group interviews'. Such techniques were used in the 1988 American Presidential election to establish the election strategy for the Republican Party. Representative groups of voters were continually being interviewed and their reactions to a number of major policy issues from both presidential nominees were monitored. The results of their reactions to these policy statements were used to strengthen or suppress aspects of the Republican policy presentation.

In any interview, the skill of the interviewer both as initiator and facilitator is of vital importance. In focus group interviews this role is called a moderator. The skills of initiating and facilitating are of particular relevance when a group of people are being simultaneously interviewed. However, as we shall see later, group interviewing is not for the novice, as even 'experts' continue to encounter many problems.

Care needs to be taken in choosing the venue for discussion. Ideally, in common with in-depth interviews, it should take place in surroundings within which the participants feel relaxed and unfrequented. This can often be on their home ground, for example in their office.

According to Walker (1985), 'the task of the group interviewer – frequently called the moderator or facilitator – is not to conduct interviews simultaneously but to facilitate a comprehensive exchange of views in which all participants are able to speak their minds and to respond to the ideas of others.' (p. 5)

Andy's experience in carrying out group interviews with lawyers (Lowe and Nilsson, 1989) endorses the view that the person carrying out the group interview (moderator) needs to be particularly skilled. He suggests the skills are essentially in two areas: initiator skills and executive skills. Initiator skills are those concerned with establishing and creating rapport before discussion takes off. Executive skills are those which give the group members sufficient confidence in the moderator to allow him or her to steer the conversation.

Andy found that for each group interview lasting about thirty minutes an additional forty minutes was taken up prior to the discussion creating an appropriate climate for the main discussion to begin. This bias of time given to preparation may feel unnaturally long to inexperienced researchers but it does reflect the importance of preparation and the time it takes for people to feel sufficiently relaxed and get the most out of the interview.

Although this type of interview is loosely structured it should never be entirely without structure. The format of the interview should be organised by using what is called a 'topic guide'. This is a résumé of the main areas of interest which are to be explored. It is designed so that, whilst still covering the general areas of interest, it should also allow unforeseen areas to emerge.

However, the problems of group interviews can sometimes outweigh the advantages. Social pressures can condition the responses gained. It may well be that people are not willing to air their views publicly. Group members often need time to be comfortable enough to speak. Our own view is that criticisms such as this illustrate the mistake of applying the wrong criteria for assessing the technique. Focus group interviews can be extremely useful in applied market research studies and are used to great effect as an exploratory tool in other types of qualitative research. Curran and Downing (1989), for example, used the technique to good effect as a means of validating the questionnaire responses made by owner/managers in a largely quantitative study which sought to understand the utility of the government's consultation strategies with small and medium sized firms.

Those wishing to know more about focus group interviewing or panel interviewing are recommended to read *Group Interviewing* by Alan Hedges (1985), which gives a clear account of how this technique might be practised and developed.

Cognitive mapping

A recent development of the group interview is known as 'cognitive mapping'. This takes an 'action research' perspective, regarding any changes in individual attitudes and organisational policies as an important part of the research process. In 'cognitive mapping' managers attempt to model the complexity of their organisational problems *as they see them* so that they can be subsequently analysed and solved.

One of the important uses of this technique has been in the area of strategy development. Originally a manual system was employed (and some still feel this is preferable since using a pen and paper keeps everything out in the open). But computer packages have also been developed (Eden, 1988a, 1988b) both to assist the analysis process as well as providing powerful support for the exploration of an organisation's strategic options. Eden argues that, for the most part, 'developing strategy has been viewed as an analytical activity devoid of urgency, fun or passion'. In addition he is critical of the traditional view that the formulation of strategy can be conducted quite independently from its implementation.

If strategic planning is actually about encouraging strategic thinking and encouraging individuals to take action, then the work of the strategic planner needs to be 'client-orientated' rather than 'plan-orientated'. Strategy formulation, therefore, needs to be seen as much as anything as a social process where the issues being dealt with are behavioural and where there is a need to understand the nature of problems, threats and opportunities as viewed or perceived by key individuals in the organisation. In Thomas and Thomas' (1928) famous words, 'If men define situations as real, they are real in their consequences.'

The approach is based on a modified form of repertory grid (see above). Senior managers who are concerned about particular problems are brought together in a room facing a large computer screen. The strategic problem or opportunity on which they are to work is presented by a member of the team. In comfortable surroundings and with a permanent supply of coffee the managers begin to consider all the aspects relating both to the existence and the solution of the problem. Each contribution made is stored by computer, and the unfolding cognitive map which represents the managers' perceptions of the problem or the opportunity is presented on the screen for them to alter and refine.

Approaches such as cognitive mapping are particularly suitable for action research designs where organisational development is an important outcome of the research. The method not only allows individual managers to offer their perceptions of a problem, but gives those responsible for strategy formulation the opportunity to understand the perspectives of others.

In this context interaction amongst participants and collaboration between researcher and researched is decidedly a good thing. The 'soft' data derived from such a technique is on many occasions the most relevant to the problems under investigation.

Researchers wishing to understand more about the techniques employed in cognitive mapping are recommended first to read

Messing about in Problems by Eden, Jones and Sims (1983), where the concept is very lucidly explained. Those wishing to read further and learn more about the process as applied to alternative decision support systems are recommended to read *Tackling Strategic Problems: The Role of Group Decision Support* (Eden and Radford, 1990).

Participant observation

The method of participant observation has its roots in ethnographic research studies, where researchers would live in tribal villages in faraway places, attempting to understand the customs and practices of strange cultures. Hence it has a very extensive literature, particularly in sociology and anthropology. Since organisations can easily be viewed as 'tribes' with their own strange customs and practices, it is by no means surprising that observation has also been used in organisational and management research. Donald Roy (1952) used the method to great effect when working as a company employee in the machine shop of a large company. He was able both to show how workers manipulated the piecework incentive scheme, and to understand the motives behind this.

The role of the participant observer is by no means simple. There are many different ways of handling it, one commonly used classification of the possibilities being that of Junkers (1960). Researchers may well come across this scheme when they read around the literature, Junkers' four main roles being; complete participation, participation as observer, observer as participant, and complete observer.

It is important for the researcher to be clear about the kind of role he is adopting, but we find that Junkers' scheme can be confusing when put into practice. Instead we propose a different scheme, based more explicitly on the possibilities available in management or organisational research. These are: researcher as employee; research as explicit role; interrupted involvement; and observation alone.

Researcher as employee
One role a researcher can take is that of employee. Here he works within the organisation, alongside others, to all intents and purposes as one of them. The role of researcher may or may not be explicit and this will have implications for the extent to which he will be able to move around and gather information and perspectives from other sources.

This role is appropriate when the researcher needs to become totally immersed and experience the work or situation at first hand. Sometimes it is the only way to gain the kind of insights sought. For example, in a study Richard conducted using this approach he was able to gain an understanding of how management's failure to cater for the workforce's motivational needs led to disillusionment and apathy (Thorpe, 1980). Poor planning of work meant that men were often bored: by experiencing this boredom himself he was better able to understand its causes and the ways in which the employees attempted to alleviate it. His team developed a pattern of activity where they worked for the first hour or so, then they took a break, had a wash and a walk outside. On certain days they changed their overalls in the laundry, which involved a walk of about 600 yards and a break of about half an hour. After mid-morning the pace became much slower, and after lunch time very little work was done at all.

One Wednesday afternoon Richard saw that the conveyor belt was beginning to back up for no apparent reason. On questioning 'colleagues' about it, he learnt that they saw this as a good way to put pressure on management and guarantee themselves overtime on Saturday morning at time and a half. Since overtime working had to be notified to the employees three days in advance it was important to slow things down on Wednesday. By Friday the backlog had all but been cleared, promising the department a fairly easy Saturday morning's work. Naturally his questioning didn't stop at just what was observed, for it then became of interest to know *why* the extra pay was required, why this strategy was used in preference to others, and so on.

In these examples, the research was conducted in a covert manner as far as the employees were concerned, but permission had been negotiated for entry via the company chairman and the works convener, who saw merits in such 'academic' research. Gaining entry had been difficult and getting both management and unions to agree had not been easy. If this had not been possible it might have been necessary to apply for, and be successful at getting, a job in the factory. This is what happened in Donald Roy's case but, in addition, in order to work in one of the company's machine shops he had first to learn to become a skilled lathe operator. Skill and competence to undertake the work or fit the role, then, is another factor that has to be considered if the researcher is to qualify for employment.

As we commented in Chapter 4, participant observation invari-ably raises *ethical* dilemmas, particularly when conducted in a covert way. These dilemmas need to be considered carefully by researchers, preferably before they embark on fieldwork. Many people are strongly resentful when they learn of the presence of a covert researcher. In Richard's own case he thought a lot about deceiving individuals whom he had begun to think of as colleagues and friends. To overcome the conflict he developed an explanation for when he was asked what he was doing, which wasn't a lie, but neither was it the whole truth.

This latter point raises another issue related to complete participation: the problem of a crisis of identity. Getting to know people quite well, even being invited into their homes, and then reporting on them in a covert way is, for most researchers, regardless of ethics, a difficult task. Richard remembers his own experience vividly. He was some 300 miles from his academic base and unable to obtain help or support from colleagues, and he found it difficult not to experience a confusion of roles. For complete participation is not just a matter of being an employee for three months or so, keeping a diary, and analysing the results at a distance at a later date. It involves observing, participating, talking, checking understanding and making interpretations, all of which are required if complete participant observers are to share and understand important parts of the employee's experience.

Linked to this is the time period over which this kind of activity has to be sustained. It is not unusual for studies to take several months, with results taking a long time to produce. It must also be noted that the method is one of high risk. As we have discussed, studies are often extremely difficult to set up, anonymity is a problem, and considerable resources may be consumed in their execution with no guarantees that the method will yield the insights sought.

Finally, and this also applies somewhat to other qualitative methodologies, the complete observer role can be a physical as well as an intellectual challenge. In Richard's case, he had to complete a day of manual work and then in the evening continue the process of interpretation so that new lines of inquiry could be continued the following day.

Research as the explicit role

A second way of managing the role is for the researcher to be present every day over a period of time, but this time entry is negotiated in advance with management and preferably with employees as well. In this case, the individual is quite clearly in the role of a researcher who can move around, observe, interview and participate in the work as appropriate.

This type of observer role is the most often favoured, as it provides many of the insights that the complete observer would gain, whilst offering much greater flexibility without the ethical problems that deception entails. Roy (1970) describes the advantages of the approach thus: 'The participant as observer not only makes no secret of his investigation: he makes it known that research is his overriding interest. He is there to observe. The participant observer is not tied down; he is free to run around as research interest beckons' (p 217).

A colleague of ours, Eileen Fairhurst (1983), used this type of approach in a study of employee's attitudes to organisational rules. She chose for her research a geriatric nursing ward, and this is where she met her first problem. It took a considerable amount of time to obtain agreement to conduct her research in a particular unit, for two reasons which illustrate a number of problems involved in this type of research. The first was that different consultants in the hospital viewed 'research' in two distinct ways. Some saw it as something in which they must become personally involved and which they must 'vet'; others saw it as a self-indulgent activity of which they wanted no part.

Even after she had gained agreement for the location of the research, there were additional problems associated with the sensitive focus of the study. Old people are especially vulnerable, and there was real concern that researching them might be viewed as a form of exploitation. To experience delay in the setting up of this kind of study is not in any way unusual. Richard's complete observer study, and the diary study that will be discussed later, took a number of months. Researchers, as we have discussed with interviewing, must find strategies that will allay people's fears, and offer the organisation or the managers and employees who control access either reassurance, or something in return. This might involve many meetings and even presentations to the employees about the aims and potential value of the research.

Once accepted, Eileen explained how a principal task was to move from a position of stranger to that of friend – someone who could be trusted. When she had achieved this she found individuals were very willing to tell her about the organisation, whether they were nurses, cleaners or ward clerks. While on the wards, Eileen felt it appropriate to help make beds and assist generally, for example, with the distribution of food and drink at meal times, and to collect bed linen or clothes for patients. At such times she was not only participating but strengthening relationships. She also recalls that there were times when she simply had to observe, for example when patients were spending time with occupational therapists or physiotherapists, or on the occasions when she did not possess the technical qualifications to take any role in the work. People understood this and accepted it.

The key skill is to be sensitive enough to know just what role is required at each particular situation. This is influenced almost entirely by the circumstances appertaining at the time. For example, Eileen explains that it would have been conspicuous if she had stood or sat rather than offered help when the wards were short staffed. On the other hand night staff were always short of work, and as a consequence she spent much of the time during this period observing, listening and talking with nurses.

Interrupted involvement
A third kind of role for the observer is for her to be present sporadically over a period of time, moving for example in and out of the organisation to deal with other work or to conduct interviews with, or observations of, different people across a number of different organisations.

The essential characteristic of the researcher taking this role is that the process is not one of continuous longitudinal involvement as we have described in the previous examples. In addition, in this case the role is unlikely to contain much actual participation in work. Instead, it provides a model for what is often seen as participant observation method: spending a period of time in a particular setting, and combining observation with interviews.

Observation alone
Finally, for completeness, we offer the role of complete observer. In many ways, this is hardly a 'qualitative' methodology, as the researcher avoids sustained interaction with those under study. This type of observation is used in the field of management services where, for job design and specification purposes, requests are made for 'objective' accounts of the content of work.

As a technique it is of absolutely no use to those interested in a social constructionist view. Even when it is used in the discipline of management services, practitioners often fail to obtain people's accounts of their own action because of their detachment. The observer role is often disliked by employees since it seems like 'eavesdropping'; the inevitable detachment prevents the degree of trust and friendship forming between researcher and respondent which, as we have noted, is an important component of the other methods.

However, for trained practitioners, such techniques do give extremely accurate pictures of what takes place and how long they take, even if they fall short of giving a full account of why things are happening.

Choice of roles

Clearly the choice of role is important. Here are some of the factors that may be taken into consideration.

1 *The purpose of the research*: does the research require continued longitudinal involvement, or will in-depth interviews conducted over time give the kind of insights required?
2 *The cost of the research*: to what extent can the researcher afford to be committed for extended periods of time, and are there any additional costs involved such as training or housing costs?
3 *The extent to which access can be gained*: gaining access where the role of the researcher is either explicit or covert, can be difficult, and may take time.
4 *The extent to which the researcher would be comfortable in the role*: if the researcher intends to keep his identity concealed, will he also feel able to develop the kind of trusting relationships that are important?
5 *The amount of time the researcher has at his disposal*: some methods involve a considerable commitment of time.

Whichever method is chosen, they all provide the means to obtain a detailed understanding of values, motives and practices. As Eileen Fairhurst comments, 'the crucial personal skill is to be seen as someone who can be trusted no matter what role is adopted – this will enable much to become possible.'

Diary methods

There is quite a long history of using diaries as a basis for social research in the UK, one of the most interesting examples being the mass-observation studies during World War II. Here a substantial number of ordinary people were recruited to keep diaries of everything they did for one day each month, and they were also asked to report on any specific days, such as bank holidays. Analysis of these diaries was intended to show how the British population in general was reacting to different aspects of the war (Calder and Sheridan, 1984).

Diaries can be either quantitative or qualitative depending on the kind of information that is recorded. They can be useful in management and organisational research on a number of levels. At one level, diaries kept by organisational members can be a simple journal or record of events. A quantitative analysis might take the form of activity sampling from which patterns may be identified statistically. This approach is sometimes used by management services practitioners who wish to measure the frequency of certain activities so that they can reorganise or 'improve' the work; sometimes it is used by managers to reflect on aspects of their own work, as in time management analysis (see, for example, Stewart, 1967, 1982). At another level, diaries might take the form of a personal journal of the research process and include a rationale for the research, emergent ideas and results, reflections on personal learning, and an examination of personal attitudes and values which may be important at the data analysis and writing up stages. At yet another level they can provide a rich qualitative picture of motives and perspectives which allows the researcher to gain considerable insight into situations being examined. It is this latter use of a diary that we wish to explore in a little more detail here.

There are a number of advantages to using diaries. Firstly, they provide a useful method for collecting data from the perspective of the employee. Whereas in participant observation the researcher cannot help imposing to some extent his own reference frame as the data is collected, in the diary study the data is collected and presented largely within the reference frame of the diary writer.

Secondly, a diary approach allows the perspectives of several different writers to be compared and contrasted simultaneously, and it allows the researcher greater freedom to move from one situation or organisation to another. Some detachment also prevents the researcher becoming too personally involved.

Thirdly, it allows the researcher to collect other relevant data while the study is in progress and enables her to carry out much more analysis than the participant observer would be able to carry out in the course of her fieldwork. This is the opportunity to collect information not only from the perspectives of different individuals, but also through using different data sources. Finally, although diary studies do not allow for the same interaction and questioning they can sometimes be an alternative to participant observation when, for example, it is impractical for a researcher to invest the time in an extended longitudinal study as observer.

A number of important lessons were learnt from a multiple diary study conducted by Richard and a colleague in one organisation during a national study into incentive schemes. Firstly, it was found to be important to select participants who were able to express themselves well in writing. In cases where a group of associates had been asked to keep a diary, and there was doubt about the competence of one person, a judgement had to be made as to the likely consequences of the individual taking offence if he was excluded.

Secondly, some structure was found necessary to give the diarist focus. To assist this a list of general headings developed from earlier pilot studies was provided. For example, the instructions for a one-day specimen diary entry enquiring into aspects of the work in a coal mine in North West England was as follows:

1 Your relationships with other people, including your supervisor, your workmates, anyone you supervise and other people you come into contact with.
2 Any particular difficulties you encountered during the day with: machinery, raw materials or other people.
3 If the incentive bonus scheme affected you at work, and if so in what way.
4 Anything you are especially pleased about or made you feel angry.
5 Anything else you feel is important, especially if it is anything to do with the incentive bonus scheme.

A third lesson it highlighted was the need for continued encouragement and reassurance during the study. An earlier pilot study had left diarists very much to their own devices, and they had continued to write for only four to six weeks. In the main study, where regular contact was maintained and feedback given in the form of additional questions or classification, almost two thirds of the sample kept writing into the third month, and more than a quarter completed the full three-month period. An improvement we might have made here would have been to supplement the diaries with interviews. This would have enhanced the effect of maintaining interest as well as providing the opportunity to probe areas of interest further.

Fourthly, the importance of the need for confidentiality was confirmed. In a pilot study, jotters had been issued to record instances that occurred during the day and this had led to problems. One particularly uncomplimentary entry in a respondent's jotter which had been left in an accessible place was read by the person described. This caused the relationships between the two people to be soured even though thoughts entered 'in the heat of the moment' did not generally reflect the opinions of the individual. It was therefore decided that even at the cost of a loss of spontaneity it was preferable for diaries to be written up away from the workplace.

Finally, the study confirmed individuals' willingness and enthusiasm for cooperating at every level. There was no evidence to justify the view that individuals might be nervous of participating in this kind of research. The experience showed that there was more nervousness among the researchers themselves, who felt that they 'dare not ask' or that asking people to maintain a diary for up to three months would be unacceptable to those under study.

All diarists in the Coal Board study to which we refer (including those who stopped writing before the end of the three-month period) maintained that they had welcomed the opportunity to express their feelings, observations and opinions about their life and work to somebody who was interested. All maintained that they enjoyed writing them, and some confided that they were flattered that outsiders were taking an interest in them as individuals. No payment or other inducements were made, although pens and folders were regularly provided. This was sufficient reward for many and it reinforces the point, made in the section on interviewing about how important it is to find out what individuals wish to gain from participating in the research.

As with participant observation, the setting up of a research study such as this involves considerable time and effort. Numerous meetings were required to gain access and our purpose had to be explained to management and union officials separately. The practicalities of undertaking diary research are fully discussed in Bowey and Thorpe (1986).

Analysing qualitative data

Methods of analysis
To some extent the issues related to the analysis of qualitative data are a microcosm of those discussed in Chapter 3 between positivist and social constructionist approaches. As one colleague once remarked 'The debate is between rigour and rigor mortis.'

If the researcher is undertaking her research from a social constructionist perspective, then she will attempt as far as is possible not to draw a distinction between the collection of data and its analysis and interpretation. Indeed, as we have discussed, the very word 'data', as something existing independently from the researcher, will be anathema. The nature of the problem being investigated and the philosophical stance taken will dictate the relationship of the research process. Exploratory research will place considerable emphasis on specifying research objectives. Research concerned with testing hypotheses will place emphasis on the data collection stage.

Secondly, within this apparently linear structure are a series of learning cycles. These have been described by Kolb (1986) as a four-stage process: concrete experience, reflective observation, abstract conceptualisation and active experimentation. For example the researcher might try out different ideas at one or a number of stages in the research process. She might then allow a period of time to elapse during which she can begin to think more clearly about the implications of her actions. The abstract conceptualisation phase is where the researcher might use wider frames of reference to illuminate what she has experienced in order to allow her intellect and creativity to externalise the ideas in new and interesting ways. Finally, during the active experimentation stage the researcher might test out these new insights or ideas and so continue round the learning cycle until a clear understanding is reached.

Many researchers after collecting qualitative data spend a great deal of time turning it into numbers or otherwise attempting to quantify it. They recognise that numbers have a seductive air and sometimes, thinking politically of the acceptability of their findings, they gear their data to quantitative statements. Others argue that doing this spoils the richness of the data, often so painstakingly collected, and fails to give the holistic view so important in qualitative research.

Even here at the analysis stage it can be seen how the philosophical links still remain, and for many managers or funders the political need for numbers wins through against the researcher's best intentions. These debates lead to two basic ways of analysing qualitative data. In one, often known as content analysis, the researcher 'goes by numbers' and 'frequency'; in the second, which we label 'grounded theory', the researcher goes by feel and intuition, aiming to produce common or contradictory themes and patterns from the data which can be used as a basis for interpretation. This second approach is much less bitty: researchers need to stay close to the data and any observations made have to be placed carefully in context. Classically, the data used in this type of research is kept out on the table and available for scrutiny. The main implications of these two approaches to data analysis are shown in Figure 5.4.

Content analysis (see also Holsti, 1969) has been used very successfully in the examination of historical artefacts. In one such study, analysis was made of Caesar's accounts of his wars in Gaul. It involved certain key phrases or words being counted, and the frequencies were then analysed. The selection of these would depend on the hypothesis the researcher wished to prove or disprove. In the case of Caesar's accounts of his campaigns the hypothesis being tested related to the forms of money being used. A similar kind of content analysis has been used to try to determine the authorship of anonymous plays and even more recently to determine where criminals' statements have been added to, or amended, by others at some later date!

Earlier in his career Richard worked in a research team that used

Content analysis	Grounded theory
Bitty	Holistic
Go by frequency	Go by feel
Objectivity	Closer to the data, open much longer
Deductive	Inductive
Testing hypotheses	Testing out themes, developing patterns

Figure 5.4 *Differences between 'content analysis' and 'grounded theory'*

a similar kind of systematic approach. Firstly, material was read and themes and statements were collected. Early problems were encountered as field notes had been used rather than verbatim tape recordings. It was therefore necessary to assume that if something had been mentioned then it had happened, if it wasn't then it hadn't. This was far from satisfactory. Secondly, three sets of interviews that were good and fat were examined by a researcher, and coding was established from key interviews. This meant that key issues the researcher wished to explore in further interviews were marked down one axis and the interviewees' numbers across the other.

Thirdly, this frame, once established, was discussed with a number of researchers and modified in the light of apparent inconsistencies. Fourthly, following the pilot study, a workshop was organised at which a number of researchers met to agree the definition of terms and the interpretation that might be placed on the three sets of interviews used. A check then showed that errors had been reduced to an acceptable level between coders.

So far at least the information had all been derived from the data, although many of the themes for which we had searched had been assessed as 'relevant' prior to analysis. Following this, all the interviews were examined for the presence of the themes which were coded on sheets for computer analysis. New themes that occurred in later interviews were handled in a flexible way and added into the framework. An example of such a framework is included in Figure 5.5. At a later date, using this method, it was possible to compare answers derived from interviews with those derived from questionnaires, moreover it was possible to separate these into definite responses and probable responses.

In some ways the method is halfway between a positivist approach and a more grounded approach. This method is commonly used when frequencies are required from qualitative or unstructured data to be added to a larger computer model; similarly when open questions occur in an otherwise structured interview or

Reasons for the introduction of an incentive scheme

Content analysis	1	2	3	4	5	6	7	8	Total
To increase profits									
To increase productivity	/	/	/	/	/	/	/	///	10
To increase production/output			/	/					2
To increase efficiency	/	/		/		/	/	++++ //	12
To increase labour flexibility								/	1
To increase earnings	//	/		/		/	/	//	8
To increase employee identification with company									
To reduce production costs									
To reduce absenteeism						/			1
To reduce wastage/rejects									
To reduce overtime									
To reduce labour turnover	/								1
Not interested									
To improve timekeeping									
To provide an incentive	/							//	3
To pay a bonus	/	/		/			/		4
To alter differentials									
To alter relativities									
To prevent industrial unrest									
To circumvent incomes policy									
Not to circumvent incomes policy									
To change production organisation									
To replace a previous scheme	/								1
To keep people employed									
To allow employee profit sharing									
To stop threatened/actual strike									
To reduce the labour force									
To get more staff									

43

Figure 5.5 *Example of content analysis coding sheet*

questionnaire, responses will be coded and added into the larger analytic framework. However, one should still remember that if this type of content analysis is undertaken, although the researcher will be able to understand what the concepts are, he will be unlikely to understand why the ideas occur and why individuals interpret things or issues in their different ways.

Grounded theory provides a more open approach to data analysis which is particularly good for dealing with transcripts. It recognises that the large amounts of non-standard data produced by qualitative studies make data analysis problematic. In quantitative data analysis an external structure is imposed on the data, which makes analysis far more straightforward. With qualitative data, however, the structure used has first to be derived from the data. This means systematically analysing it so as to tease out themes, patterns and categories. As Jones (1987) comments, grounded theory works because 'rather than forcing data within logico-deductively derived assumptions and categories, research should be used to generate grounded theory, which "fits" and "works" because it is derived from the concepts and categories used by social actors themselves to interpret and organise their worlds' (p. 25).

We discussed the approach of Glaser and Strauss (1967) above in Chapter 3. This has been taken further by researchers such as Turner (1981, 1983) and we find his method useful in processing and sifting through volumes of non-standard data. In order to make the procedure more understandable we explain it in the following way, based on personal experiences and those of our colleagues. The method assumes that one is working with transcripts of in-depth interviews – one of the more intractable analysis problems. We consider that there are seven main stages to such analysis:

1 Familiarisation: Re-read the data transcripts again. Doing this will enable some first thoughts to emerge: be aware and notice interesting things. When reading, draw on unrecorded information as well as recorded. This is where the filed notes and personal diary come into the analytic process. Note should be taken of, for example, the relationships established between the researcher and the people interviewed, the general attitude of the respondent, and the level of confidence felt about the data that was offered, Nuances and intonation may also be important at this stage, so going back to the recorded interviews and listening to them again may be important.

The researcher may begin to doodle or jot down some first ideas. The stage however is essentially exploratory, where questions begin to be framed.

2 Reflection: At this stage desperation may begin to set in. There is usually so much rich data that trying to make sense of it seems an impossible task. Often researchers find that they have missed some crucial issues which should have been explored, but which for some reason were not. A process of evaluation and critique becomes more evident as the data is evaluated in the light of previous research, academic texts and common sense explanations. The kind of questions that researchers might ask themselves are:

Does it support existing knowledge?
Does it challenge it?
Does it answer previously unanswered questions?
What is different?
Is it different?

In order to undertake this stage successfully it is often necessary to be aware of previous research, models and ideas. Cataloguing is important here so that previous research can be considered and evaluated. Ideas begin to be formulated and reformulated in the light of previous work. It is helpful if researchers begin to talk to other researchers or supervisors about provisional thoughts, hypotheses or ideas. This is a good way of 'testing the water' with an idea or emerging pattern.

The stage is distinctive for the volume and range of hypotheses, explanations or solutions which are still very much at the instinctive 'gut feelings' stage. These still need thinking about and might be substantiated, but haven't yet been rigorously tested.

3 Conceptualisation: At this stage there is usually a set of concepts or variables which seem to be important for understanding what is going on. For example, in an examination of performance these might include: management style, technology, absence rates, demographic qualities of the labour force, locus of power and so on. These concepts which respondents mentioned are now articulated as explanatory variables.

However, at this stage the researcher will not be sure just how reliable or valid these concepts are: do they really relate in a consistent way to how the individual views an issue, or has there been misinterpretation of what has been said? What is needed, therefore, is for the researcher to go back to the data and search for them, methodically highlighting them when they appear. There

are a number of different ways this can be done but we find that
different coloured pens are a useful device, or one can write code
words in the enlarged right hand margin of the transcript.

At this stage the researcher may well come across more concepts
which were previously missed, and these can be added to the list.

4 Cataloguing concepts: Once it is established that the concepts
identified do seem to occur in people's explanations, then they can
be transferred onto cards as a quick reference guide. When this is
done there is an issue of labelling. Do you use the language of the
people concerned when labelling or do you use your own terms?
Our view is that it is probably helpful at this stage to use your own
terms, providing a trace is kept of how they were derived.

One way in which it can be achieved is by using a card index in
which the concepts on, say, labour turnover are written down. The
entry on the card needs to give the reference to its source in the
transcripts, and it may be further elaborated with a word or phrase
which indicates the content. Figure 5.6 shows an example of such
a card.

However, it should be noted that, although it is systematically
seductive, not everyone agrees that this is always a good approach.
Writing on cards, or using a computer database (which we discuss
later), tends to mechanise what ought to be an intuitive process,
thus damaging the power of explanation and in a sense acquiescing
to the need to 'play the game'. Even Turner (1981) concedes that
the intuitive approach can produce 'brilliant material' and suggests
that the card approach might be more suited to beginners to ensure
that nothing is missed out.

5 Recoding: Now that all the references to particular concepts
are known, it will be possible to go back quickly and easily to those
places in the data to see what was actually said. It may, for example, be noticed that some concepts were used within different
contexts or were used to explain different phenomena. Similarly, it
may be found that what the respondent meant by a particular
concept was different to what was understood by it. Or that
different people in the same organisation were defining differently
what appear at face value to be similar concepts. It may even be
the case that there are just too many concepts/variables to be
manageable. This is an indication that the coding framework might
be too refined, but an equal danger is that it is too crude, or too
simplistic. For any of these reasons recoding will be necessary.
When any recoding is undertaken, interpretation and analysis also
take place.

Labour turnover

Interview	Page	Line	
4	3	7	Others' motives
11	2	18	Effect on production
4	9	23	Management policies

Figure 5.6 *Index card for cataloguing concepts in interviews*

For example, it may be the case that a number of people used the concept of flexibility as an explanation for why their organisation survived the recession in the early 1980s. But on probing what people meant by flexibility, it might be found that some people were talking about labour mobility, some were talking about flexible working hours, while others were talking about flexibility in strategic directions.

So, at this stage, concepts are beginning to be redefined and recoded. As we indicated earlier it may well prove necessary to collapse some of the codes used into more general ones. This is called laddering. Laddering can take place both up and down – that is by enlarging or collapsing codes.

6 Linking: By now the analytical framework and explanations should be becoming clearer, with patterns emerging and concepts spotted that could fit together. There should be a clearer hypothesis based on the evidence which has been gathered and organised. One can now begin to link all the variables which have been identified as important into a more holistic theory. This involves linking empirical data with more general models and it takes the form of tacking backwards and forwards between the literature and the evidence collected in practice.

This stage often produces a first draft which can be used to try out on others, thus exposing the argument and data to scrutiny. It is important therefore that this draft is presented to others, either to colleagues in the field, or to the respondents themselves.

7 Re-evaluation: In the light of the comments of others, the researcher may feel that more work is needed in some areas. For example, the analysis may have omitted to take account of some factors or have over-emphasised others. Following a consideration of issues such as these the first draft is rewritten, taking into account the criticisms made and contradictions highlighted. This stage may go on for a considerable period of time, and as with the other stages it may have to be undertaken more than once.

This approach can be applied to almost any kind of qualitative data. As with other methods of data collection a critical peer group of researchers can be useful in the early stages of research to suggest new categories as well as assist with interpretation of the data. The researcher may well feel that for much of the time the analysis of qualitative data is chaotic and extremely messy. A colleague of Richard's had his dining room out of commission for some four weeks whilst cards littered the table and floor and covered the walls. The themes he developed as a result were well worth the inconvenience. Bott (1971) has noted that 'one is caught in a dilemma between succumbing to confusion or choosing some simple, plausible but false explanation. We decided to succumb to confusion in the hope that it would be temporary.'

As with many systematic approaches, the method outlined is not without its critics. It can be argued that the systematic nature of the process to provide rigour for academic 'peer' assessment does harm to itself and in a sense becomes a reductionist approach. The argument is that research and analysis in qualitative data is about 'feel' and an implicit component of all research is the honesty of the person conducting the research. Researchers wishing to learn more about this process should read Turner, (1981) or Jones 'The Analysis of Depth Interviews' in Walker (1985).

Analysing structured interviews or questionnaires

The procedure outlined above is useful for a large volume of unstructured, in-depth data. The approach is time consuming and costly, and requires verbatim transcripts to be available.

But in applied research, especially where a large number of interviews may have been conducted by different people, a less time consuming and more standardised approach is necessary. This must allow the researcher to draw key features out of the data, whilst at the same time allowing the richness of some of the material to remain for illustration purposes.

Miles and Huberman (1984) put forward a method of analysing qualitative data that is both simple and rigorous. For the method to be used effectively, the data needs to have been collected by means of a semi-structured questionnaire where respondents have been allowed to write their views on a number of open questions, or by means of a semi-focused interview as described by Merton and Kendal (1957). These methods are used when the researcher feels she knows fairly well what she is after but sees that a greater insight might be gained from permitting the respondent to choose his own path. The broad parameters though are very clearly set by the researcher.

In this type of analysis conceptual frameworks are encouraged and are used as boundary devices that need not work as strait jackets (Miles and Huberman, 1984: 29). Further, these frameworks can be revised to make them more precise as the research progresses.

Analysis of the data resulting from this method of inquiry is generally accomplished by drawing up the questions on a specially prepared matrix or analysis sheet. All the specific questions are drawn up along the top of the page, and the respondents are identified down one margin. The researcher then works through each interview or questionnaire in turn, cataloguing the various responses made to the main themes for which information is sought. What emerges from such analysis are visual patterns or themes that can either be qualified by reference to the individual transcripts, or quantified if numbers permit he use of statistical treatments. Those wishing to explore the various ways in which this might be done in relation to the particular focus of their study are recommended to read Miles and Huberman (1984).

The use of computers with qualitative data

Computers have recently established themselves as key aids in qualitative data handling and analysis. However, we must stress that we are sceptical of many of the computer packages available for qualitative research; and there is no package that can substitute for the interpretive skills of the researcher. Many of them can alleviate much of the clerical task of sorting words, concepts and passages contained in the transcripts; but the identification of significant themes, patterns and categories still has to be done by the researcher.

Available packages can be grouped into distinct types; these range from familiar word processing packages, through various forms of databases, to the potential (as yet largely unrealised) of expert systems. We comment briefly below on the nature of some of these packages, and on their limitations.

Word processing packages are very widely used for storing notes and other forms of data. The availability of small portable computers means that data can now be entered directly into a memory while attending meetings or conducting fieldwork. Notes can be elaborated subsequently, and analysis can be aided by inserting code names into the text which classify and label particular forms of information. The search and retrieve options in the word processing package can then be used to locate and group material around the themes identified. The main limitation of these packages is that the search/retrieve process is slow and sequential, and it is not possible to sort within more than one theme at once.

A recent development is *'hypertext programs'*, which add some of the features of databases onto word processing packages. Once data has been entered into the computer the program allows the text to be 'tagged' with invisible markers, and it is possible to develop complex trails of markers throughout the text which can be reviewed very flexibly. Although enormous benefits are claimed by the producers of this kind of software it is not yet clear whether these are fully justified.

A third approach is provided by *'text-based database programe'*. These differ from traditional database programs in that they allow large amounts of text in any field (perhaps 30,000 characters, rather than 1,000 characters), and they provide text editing facilities rather like a word processor. Editing, searching and analysis of data can be done very easily with these packages. The main drawbacks are that all data needs to be contained within the same field, which can produce storage problems, and the inflexibility of the overall framework within which the data is classified. This latter can be a significant limitation when handling qualitative data in an exploratory way. It is also possible to use more traditional databases (such as dBase IV) with qualitative data if one wishes to assess the frequency with which particular qualities occur. This process is known as 'enumerative induction' and can provide a useful complement to purer forms of qualitative analysis.

Finally, there is the possibility of developing *expert systems* to work with qualitative data. Here you have to bear in mind that the expert system cannot do the thinking for you. The main difference between an expert system and the packages described above is that it is constructed around associations in the data rather than as a straight repository of data. The system is capable of providing logical answers to questions asked of it based only on the associations already programmed by the researcher. In practice expert systems work well within very narrow areas of knowledge. This is because the contextual associations required to answer questions increase geometrically as the breadth of the questions increases arithmetically. Thus, although they may be of value in highly specialised areas, expert systems are unlikely to become of general relevance to qualitative researchers for some time to come.

In addition to the above there are a number of other packages that may help qualitative analysis in certain circumstances. These include indexing systems, concordance programs and 'idea processing software'. These are described and assessed in Pfaffenberger (1988), which represents one of the most accessible overviews of this subject.

In conclusion we feel it is important to emphasise four general points about the use of computers for analysing qualitative data. Firstly, they always depend on the judgement of the researcher, and cannot substitute for this. Secondly, packages and programs need to be chosen for, and be appropriate to, the tasks required. Thirdly, remember that it may often be much easier to analyse qualitative data by hand; and finally, beware of the possibility that the availability of computer analysis may lead to an emphasis on counting the frequency of categories, at the expense of understanding the *quality* of ideas and experiences.

Conclusion

In this chapter we have attempted to provide an overview of some of the main ways of capturing qualitative data and making sense of it. A commitment to qualitative research is likely to derive from the researcher's view about which features of the world are significant and relevant to his enterprise. The key question is whether the quality of experience is more important than the frequency of opinions and events.

As we indicated in Part Two, this choice is likely to be influenced by many other factors, including the nature of the research focus, and the politics of research funding and of individual careers. On the other hand the choice of methodological stance will constrain the uses to which research may be put. It is likely that qualitative research will relate to the needs and interests of those being researched. But this is by no means inevitable: it depends on the purpose and ethical positions of those conducting and sponsoring research.

Along the road of qualitative research there are also many dilemmas. There is the problem of public access to private experiences, and the difficulty of deciding how and when to impose any interpretive frameworks on this. There is the question of how accurate one's information is, and how 'accurate' it needs to be, or can be. And there is the continual tension underneath the research process between creating meanings and counting frequencies. In the next chapter we consider some of the methods and issues associated with the latter problem.

6
Quantitative Methods

In this chapter we review some of the more important quantitative techniques of data collection and analysis. Although the emphasis of the book has been on the use of qualitative methods, it seems important to provide some coverage of quantitative methods both to illustrate the possibilities and problems of these methods, and to show the contrast with qualitative methods.

As we have explained in the previous chapter the distinction between quantitative and qualitative techniques is not always clear. Some techniques, such as interviews, can be used to gather data in either a quantitative or a qualitative way; similarly, a single piece of data, such as an interview transcript, can be analysed in either way. But there are a number of other techniques, such as psychological tests, or activity sampling, which tend to be used predominantly in quantitative ways. One important feature of quantitative techniques is that the process of data collection becomes distinct from analysis. Hence the chapter is organised into two main sections according to this distinction.

In the section on data collection we concentrate primarily on the design of questionnaires, and on survey methods which make extensive use of questionnaires. In the second section we will look at different ways of summarising different forms of quantitative data – and making some sense of it. We conclude with some thoughts on the possibilities of using different kinds of methods within the same study.

Data collection

We distinguish four main ways of gathering quantitative data: interviews, questionnaires, tests/measures, and observation. Information can also be gathered from archives and databanks, although this seems more straightforward because data is already in existence and does not need to be 'created' by the researcher in the same way as the responses to an interview are created.

The emphasis will be placed on questionnaires because most of the general issues of quantitative techniques can be illustrated with them, but we start with some brief comments on each of the other techniques.

Interviews are often used in market research or opinion polls to gather quantitative data. In this case the interviewer will have a series of precisely worded questions (such as 'when did you last travel on a train?'), and will expect to receive either a factual answer ('Last Thursday'), or a less precise answer ('Oh, I think it must have been a few months ago'). Where the answer is likely to be imprecise, as is often the case with matters of opinion, the interviewer will be furnished with four or five alternative answers, into which she, or the interviewee, is expected to fit the response. Each alternative response will have been given a numerical code, so that the whole interview can be recorded as a series of numbers. It is possible to carry out these interviews either face-to-face or over the telephone. Although most people are prepared to answer three or four questions without prior warning, interviews that will last any longer need to be 'legitimised' by someone like a works manager, and arranged in advance. Even if the interview is highly 'structured' it should still be remembered that the interaction is a social process. During the interview the respondent will be sizing up the interviewer, and responses may well be affected by the inferences drawn. Factors such as gender, social class, age and apparent motives are likely to have an influence on the data provided. Accuracy can be increased if the interviewer avoids stating her own views, phrases questions impartially, and appears equally accepting of any answer (Moser and Kalton, 1971). The only problem with this is that the interviewee may feel the interaction is 'phoney', and therefore become less prepared to cooperate.

Tests and measures can be used to find out how, or what, the individual thinks. In most cases they take the form of a series of written questions (50–100) with Yes/No answers. The pattern of answers given by an individual can be compared with the patterns of answers given by past respondents to see whether she is normal or abnormal in certain respects. The term 'abnormal' is, of course, being used in a statistical sense here to indicate that a particular response is unusual, and contains no implications of whether the response is right or wrong.

Personality tests, such as Eysenck's EPI or Cattell's 16-PF, are claimed to be 'objective' in several senses (Eysenck and Eysenck, 1973; Cattell and Warburton, 1967). They have no implications for which answers are right or wrong; the scores produced by an individual on different occasions are fairly constant; it is very difficult for the respondent to 'fake' a particular result; and the person who administers the test is assumed to have minimal influence on the results. Thus, for the psychologist they have the attraction of providing measures of human characteristics with an accuracy that approximates measures in the natural sciences. Tests are used very extensively within organisations, although normally where a power differential exists: say, by the recruitment manager on the job applicant, by the management development manager on the ambitious junior manager, or by the therapist on the patient.

In educational settings tests may also be used in a self-diagnostic sense to help the individual identify his own 'learning style' (Honey and Mumford, 1982) or natural 'team role' (Belbin, 1981). These tests are less elaborate and 'objective' than the ones mentioned above, but they have the advantage of being more open to the respondent and they do not rely totally on the expert to unravel their mysteries. The other forms of test that are used very frequently in educational settings are *attainment* and *intelligence* tests which measure attributes such as reading performance, mathematical ability, aptitude for conducting graduate management studies (GMAT), and so on. These tend to be used diagnostically, or to aid the decision-making of teachers.

Observation, although most often used as a qualitative technique, can also be standardised and systematised in a highly quantitative way. This is the technique of Activity Sampling, which is extensively used in work study and operations management (Currie, 1959). Instant observations are made at regular intervals of processes or individuals at work. The nature of activity or process is classified and recorded at each observation time, and over a period of time the frequency of each category is calculated as a percentage of all the activities observed.

This approach to observation is very useful in understanding how individuals spend their time, in reviewing the allocation of resources, or in assessing the frequency of delays. The advantages of the method are that observations can be made by relatively untrained observers, observations can be carried out simultaneously or over a long period, and in order to increase accuracy one simply needs to increase the number of observations. On the other hand care needs to be taken in the allocation of observation times to ensure that results are not unduly dominated by unrepresentative periods of the day. For this reason it is often worth conducting a preliminary study so that one can be confident that the observation programme is feasible and unlikely to produce bias.

Finally there are *written records and indices*. House journals, internal reports, memoranda, Chairman's statements, and newspaper articles have always provided good material for the qualitative researcher. But the development of public databases, such as DATASTREAM, now provides instant access to quantitative indicators of corporate performance. The main limitation of this kind of data is that it is constructed at a 'macro' level, regarding each company as a single entity. Researchers who are more interested in internal quantitative indicators will need to look for management control data, which may be easy to come by if one is already an employee of the organisation.

Questionnaires

Questionnaires are very widely used in large scale investigations of political opinions and consumer preferences. Although they may seem simple to use and analyse, their design is by no means simple. A number of sources are worth consulting. The 'classic' books by Oppenheim (1966) and Moser and Kalton (1971) still give very good advice, even if their examples are looking a bit dated; more recent, and very practical, guidance is provided by Youngman (1984). The main decisions to be made in questionnaire design relate to the type of questions to be included and the overall format of the questionnaire.

Question types Firstly we distinguish between questions of 'fact' and questions of 'opinion'. For example, biographical details such as age, level of education or length of service are reasonably factual: the respondent may still choose to give incorrect answers, but there still exists, in most cases, a correct answer. With questions of opinion there can be no assumption about underlying correct answers; indeed, they are useful precisely because people will respond to them in different ways. Secondly, there is the distinction between 'open' and 'closed' questions. If, for example, one wished to find out how a manager felt about her company as an employer, an open question might ask: 'In what respects is this company a good employer?' – to which the answer would be a written statement, perhaps a couple of lines long. A closed question with the same focus might be: 'Do you consider this company to be a good employer?' – and the response would be limited to circling either a 'Yes' or a 'No'.

It is also possible to construct open questions which provide some structure to the answers: 'List, in order, the three things you like most about this company as an employer.' And closed questions can be constructed to allow more discrimination than a straight Yes/No choice. One of the most common forms is known as a Likert scale and illustrated in Figure 6.1. The respondent will be asked to ring one answer category indicating the strength of agreement or disagreement with the initial statement. Another form of closed question which still requires the exercise of

This company is a good employer: Agree strongly   1
                                    Agree   2
                                    Undecided   3
                                    Disagree   4
                                    Strongly disagree   5

Figure 6.1   *Example of a Likert scale*

judgement is the ranking exercise, where the respondent is asked to indicate the order of importance or value of a list of attributes or statements. Given the complexity of ranking long lists of items it is normally advisable to restrict the number of items to about six.

The strength of closed questions is that they are quick to complete and analyse; the weakness is that the data obtained may be very superficial. Open questions allow the possibility of asking deeper questions and obtaining unanticipated perspectives on an issue, but the corresponding weakness is that completion and analysis can be difficult and time consuming. There are a number of general principles to consider when drafting items for a questionnaire. These are:

1 Make sure that the question is clear.
2 Avoid any jargon or specialist language.
3 Avoid 'personal' questions.
4 Don't ask two questions in one item.
5 Avoid 'leading' questions which suggest indirectly what the right answer might be.

Questionnaire layout   It is important that questionnaires are well produced, and that they seem easy to complete. Sometimes, especially with open questions, the respondent may get so interested that he will willingly devote a lot of time to it. But the principle remains the same: the benefits of completing the questionnaire should outweigh the costs measured by time or inconvenience. Unfortunately managers seem to be increasingly busy nowadays, so their time is becoming more and more valuable.

Although the formatting and layout of questionnaires may be considered something of an art, there are still some widely accepted principles of good practice. These include:

1 Provide a short covering letter explaining the purpose of the research and why/how the respondent was selected.
2 Start the questionnaire with brief instructions about how to complete it.
3 Vary the type of question occasionally, but keep similar types of question together in bunches.

4 Start with simpler factual questions, moving on later to items of opinion or values.

In addition it is worth considering photo-reducing the questionnaire so it does not appear too daunting to the respondent, and differentiating between instructions and questions by varying the typeface between italic and roman.

Sometimes it is possible to borrow items and portions of questionnaires from other sources, especially when a lot of prior questionnaire-based research exists into concepts such as motivation, or organisational climate. But however good the design, or prior testing of question, it is always advisable to 'pilot' the questionnaire on a small number of people before using it 'for real'. This enables one to check that the items are easily understood and that there are no obvious problems to do with length, sequencing of questions, sensitive items, etc. It is also most important at this stage to see whether it is possible to analyse the data produced by the questionnaire . . . and whether the results appear to make any sense.

Reliability and validity We discussed in Chapter 3 the importance attached to ensuring validity and reliability when gathering quantitative data. Validity is a question of how far we can be sure that a test or instrument measures the attribute which it is supposed to measure. This is not too easy to ascertain, because if one already had a better way of measuring the attribute, there would be no need for a new instrument. In this context, George Kelly is reported to have defined validity as 'the capacity of a test to tell us what we already know' (Bannister and Mair, 1968).

Nevertheless there are various ways of estimating validity (Patchen, 1965):

Face validity:	whether the instrument or its items are plausible
Convergent validity:	confirmation by comparing the instrument with other independent measurement procedures
Validation by known groups:	comparing groups otherwise known to differ on the factor in question

Reliability is primarily a matter of stability: if an instrument is administered to the same individual on two different occasions, will it yield the same result? The main problem with testing this in practice is that no one can be sure that the individual, and other factors, have not changed between the two occasions.

Hence it is more common to examine 'equivalence reliability', which is the extent to which different items intended to measure the same thing correlate with each other.

Ideally, tests for validity and reliability should be made at the pilot stage of an investigation, before the main phase of data collection. Responses to items are correlated with each other along the lines indicated above to provide reliability coefficients and indications of the accuracy of the results that might be produced. We discuss correlations later in this chapter, but can note here that for exploratory research reliability coefficients in the order of 0.6 are acceptable, but psychological tests designed for public use world require coefficients of around 0.9.

Surveys

Questionnaires and interviews are used extensively in surveys. Occasionally tests and observations are included, but they are more frequently used to aid decisions about individuals, or as an element of experiments. We have discussed these briefly in Chapter 5, and propose to focus here on survey methods, particularly when they rely on questionnaires or structured interviews.

The main purposed of a survey is to obtain information from, or about, a defined set of people, or 'population'. This population might be defined to include: all the people in one country; all women aged between 30 and 40 who live in Paris; all managers of Grade 7 or above who work for the Pirelli organisation; or all supervisors in a company who have attended course Y during the last 3 years. When the population is small (perhaps less than 500) it is customary to send the questionnaire to all members. This 100% sample is known as a 'census'. In the case of structured interviews the size of sample is limited by the time available to interviewers, and with qualitative questionnaires it is limited by the feasibility of coding and analysis. But with quantitative questionnaires the sky is the limit given some help from the postal system, the storage capacity of the computer, and the skills of data processing staff.

However, it is not always necessary to contact everyone in a population in order to know what they think, and this is where sampling methods come in. The main aim of sampling is to construct a sub-set of the population which is fully representative in the main areas of interest. It is then possible to infer statistically the likelihood that a pattern observed in the sample will also be replicated in the population.

The simplest form of sample is the *random* sample. Here every 'unit' of the population has an equal chance of being selected for the sample, and this can be done by using a table of random numbers, by picking out every fifth name on a list of employees, by taking the first name on every right hand page of the telephone directory, or whatever. If some key features of the population are already known it is possible to take some short cuts. For example, one might wish to compare the attitudes of supervisors and middle managers towards their company. If there are 1,000 middle managers and 5,000 supervisors one might choose to sample 20% of the middle managers and 10% of the supervisors. This would give respective sub-sample sizes of 200 and 500 individuals, both of which are reasonable numbers (we give further guidance on sample sizes below). This would form a *stratified sample*, and individuals would be selected at random within each of these strata. If wished, further strata could be included in the sample, such as departments or gender, provided they contained mutually exclusive categories; but if the process of stratification is continued too far one can end up with tiny groups that may not be representative of anything.

Two other forms of sampling which produce less representative pictures than the above methods are quota and cluster samples. With a *quota sample* there is no attempt to randomise selection. For example the instruction might be to: 'interview the first 20 people wearing bowler hats who enter the station after 8.00 am'. Interviews continue until the quota has been filled, then they stop. The method can easily introduce bias into the sample if, continuing the above example, all the bowler-hatted men entering the station between 8.00 and 9.00 are businessmen, and those entering the station after 9.00 are politicians. *Cluster sampling* has similar limitations because it involves taking all members of a unit, say Departments 3 and 6 in a factory containing 10 departments. The main advantage of both these methods is that they are comparatively cheap. For those wishing to look further at issues of sampling, a useful reference would be Sudman (1976).

Sample size and accuracy
The question everybody asks is 'how big a sample do I need?' The good news is that there is an answer to this question; the bad news is that the answer depends on already knowing a lot about the population to be investigated, and it may also vary with the question asked. The formula to use is:

$$n = \frac{P(100 - P)}{E^2}$$

where n is the sample size required, P is the percentage occurrence of the state or condition, and E is the maximum error required.

For example, if one item in a questionnaire asked workers in a factory whether they were satisfied, and it provided a Yes/No answer, we could use the formula to determine how many responses would be required to produce a standard error[1] of, say, no more than 5%. The one snag is that we would still have to estimate the likelihood that workers would answer Yes or No. If we guessed, perhaps as a result of a quick pilot study, that 60% would say yes, we could now use the formula as follows:

$$n = \frac{60(100 - 60)}{5^2} = 96$$

That would give us the minimum sample required to provide 95% accuracy for that one question.

With a questionnaire containing many such items the calculation would need to be carried out several times to get a feel for the range of sample sizes indicated. But as a quick rule of thumb, provided the distributions of responses to each question are fairly well balanced, then:

$$n = \frac{2500}{E^2}$$

Three further factors can be considered which have different effects on the required sample size. Firstly, if the population is not much greater than n, the sample size does not have to be so large in order to provide an accurate estimate of features of the population. The formula for reducing n (known as the *finite population correction*) is:

$$n' = \frac{n}{1 + \dfrac{n}{N}}$$

---

[1] The terms (standard) error and accuracy are used here according to their statistical meanings. Technically the standard error is the standard deviation of estimates of the population mean produced by random samples of the size indicated. In practice this implies that on approximately 95% of occasions the estimate of a mean provided by the sample (say, the average age of employees) will be within two standard errors of the true population mean. Both error and accuracy are expressed in percentage terms, and they add up to 100%. (See Maxwell, 1970: 52–9, for further discussion of this point.)

where n is the sample size indicated above,
N is the total population size, and
n' is the reduced sample required.

Thus, if the population was five times n (in our example), then

$$n' = \frac{96}{1 + \dfrac{96}{480}} = 80$$

Now the downside. The above discussion has assumed that the full sample size will be available for analysis. If, however, this is a questionnaire distributed by internal mail to members of a company it could be unreasonable to expect a response rate of more than 50%. Thus, in order to ensure that an adequate number of questionnaires are returned for analysis, the number dispatched would need to be doubled (to 160), at least.

Thirdly, we have assumed in our calculations that the selection of sample members has been truly random, and that all are equally likely to respond, or not respond. But because of some of the factors discussed in the previous section it is quite likely that the sample is not truly representative of the population. Equally there may be considerable bias produced by non-response. If the survey is about job satisfaction it may well be that the least satisfied people will not respond, thus biasing the overall response towards a more positive picture. There are no statistical solutions to this problem other than increasing the overall sample to provide a greater margin of safety, or conducting an additional survey of those who don't respond. Of course, the latter will only be possible if all questionnaires are identifiable – and identification could produce yet another source of bias.

Data analysis

Types of quantitative data
Before attempting any form of quantitative analysis it is important to be clear about the kind of data involved. Three main kinds of data are encountered in management research: nominal, ordinal and interval.

Nominal data implies no more than a labelling of different categories. The gender classifications, male/female, or occupational classifications such as lawyer, artist, engineer, teacher, etc, would provide nominal data; there is no obvious ordering of these categories. But if we used classifications of social class, or responses to a questionnaire item which offered a range of answers (such as, strongly agree, agree, neither agree nor disagree, disagree, strongly disagree), it would be possible to place all of the classifications in order. Consequently this would be known as *ordinal data*. Although it is possible to say with social class classifications that Class 1 is above Class 2, and so on, it is hard to claim that the difference between Class 1 and Class 2, however defined, is the same as the difference between Class 3 and Class 4. A similar point applies with the questionnaire responses: one cannot be sure that the difference between 'agree' and 'strongly agree' is the same as the difference between 'neither agree nor disagree' and 'agree'. It is only with classifications such as age, weight or salary that the interval between any one pair of points, say, 25 years and 30 years, is the same as the interval between any other pair of points, say, 47 years and 52 years. This is what is known as *interval data*.

Descriptive statistics

The distinction between types of data is most important when statistics are used to summarise features of the sample. With interval data it is possible to use 'parametric' statistics such as measures of mean, standard deviation and variance to summarise key features of the data. When the data is merely ordinal it is usually necessary to use 'non-parametric' statistics, which do not assume equal intervals between successive points on a scale. The simplest of these are frequency counts, and indicators of averages such as medians and modes. The 'mean' is obtained arithmetically by adding up all the scores in a sample and dividing by the total number in the sample; the median is the middle number, and the mode is the most frequent number. For example, if the ages of a group of students in a class are:

21, 21, 21, 21, 22, 23, 24, 24, 26, 26, 28
the mean is 257/11 = 23.4 years,
the median is 23 years, and
the mode is 21 years.

Here the mean is probably the most useful description of the average age in this group, although there are occasions (say, if one member of the group had been aged 74) where the arithmetic mean might be more misleading, and the median would provide a better indication of the average age.

If, however, one wished to summarise the distribution of social class in the group and the eleven students were classified as follows on an A to D system:

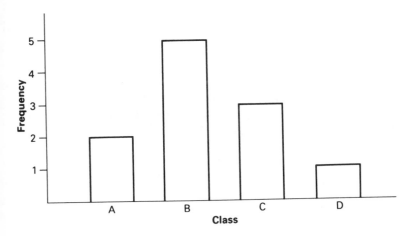

Figure 6.2 *Histogram*

B B A D C C A B B C B

this would have to be summarised as a frequency count:

Class	Frequency
A	2
B	5
C	3
D	1

or as a histogram (Figure 6.2). Clearly the most frequent class (mode) is Class B, and the middle case (median) is also in Class B.

However, it is often tempting to go further by treating ordinal data as if it was interval data and hence use parametric statistics on it. Thus the four social classes above might have been expressed as Classes 1 to 4, and one could then produce an arithmetic mean for the group, $25/11 = 2.27$. Exactly what is meant by Class 2.27 is another matter; but this procedure is often used to summarise the results of Likert scales (see Figure 6.1 above). This is, strictly speaking, incorrect; but with a large sample and a continuous dimension such as 'strongly agree' to 'strongly disagree' the result is often both accurate and useful.

Other statistics that are useful for describing parametric data are the standard deviation and variance. The standard deviation of a variable is given by the formula:

$$s = \sqrt{\frac{\Sigma(\bar{x}-x_i)^2}{n-1}}$$

where x_i is the score for the ith person, $\bar{x}$ is the arithmetic mean for that variable, and n is the number in the sample. This is fairly easy to work out manually for a small sample, although scientific calculators and statistical packages provide short cuts. In the case of the above data about ages of students the calculation runs:

$$s = \sqrt{\frac{(23.4-21)^2}{11-1}+\frac{(23.4-21)^2}{11-1}+\ldots+\frac{(23.4-28)^2}{11-1}}$$

$$= \sqrt{\frac{5.76}{10}+\frac{5.76}{10}+\ldots+\frac{21.6}{10}}$$

$$= \sqrt{\frac{60.56}{10}} = 2.46$$

This indicates the extent to which the scores on the variable are bunched together; the higher the standard deviation, the more dispersed they are. The other term, variance, is simply the square of the standard deviation: 6.05 in this case.

Measures of similarity and difference
Although simple descriptive statistics are a useful preliminary, it is often more interesting for research purposes to show that one group of people, or objects, is similar to, or different from, another group. This is particularly so where, in the more positivist forms of research, one wishes to establish the causes and effects of different factors. For example, one might want to know whether the presence, or absence, of a new incentive scheme would have any effect on the morale or productivity of workers in a factory.

There are many statistical techniques, both parametric and non-parametric, for demonstrating similarities and differences in data. These are available on most statistical packages (see below), and technical details are covered fully in the accompanying manuals. Two good books for further reading on this topic are Maxwell (1970), mainly on parametric statistics, and Siegel (1956), which provides comprehensive treatment on non-parametric statistics. In this section we mention briefly some of the more useful tests.

Firstly, similarity is most commonly demonstrated using correlation statistics. This requires variables to be matched, item by item,

	Salary		Total
	Under £25k	£25k or over	
Male	18	15	33
Female	13	4	17
Total	31	19	50

Figure 6.3 *Contingency table*

as would be the case, if, say, the relationship between salary and physical height was being investigated across a sample of 50 managers. For each manager there would be two scores, height and salary, and the statistic would measure how far high scores on one were associated with high or low scores on the other. The *product moment correlation coefficient* is most commonly used with parametric data. With non-parametric data there are a number of tests such as Kendall Tau or Spearman Rho (Siegel, 1956) which are based on the rank order of scores rather than the absolute numeric scores themselves. Correlation coefficients vary between -1 and $+1$, which indicate total negative and positive correlations respectively, and the mid-point, zero, indicates no relationship whatever.

Tests of difference can either be applied to attributes of individuals or objects, or to groups as a whole. If the aim was to assess whether male managers in a company have higher salaries than female managers at equivalent levels, one measure would be an analysis of variance. This test assesses whether the dispersion (variance) in salaries for the male and female groups together is large in comparison with the variance within each separate group. A large common variance combined with low variance in the separate groups would indicate that the difference is quite important.

Another useful way of examining differences or associations between groups, especially when the factor under investigation can be reduced to a few nominal categories, is the *chi-square* test. This can be done manually in most cases so we shall give a brief example of the calculation here.

First it is necessary to draw up the data in a contingency table. This, for the above example with gender and salary, could look like Figure 6.3, where the numbers in each box indicate how many managers fall into that category.

The formula for the chi-square test is:

$$\chi^2 = \sum \frac{(O-E)^2}{E}$$

where O is the observed (actual) number of cases falling into that category

E is the expected number of cases falling into that category.

E is calculated for each category as the product of the column and row subtotals divided by the full total. Thus for 'males, under £25K' the expected frequency would be:

$$\frac{33 \times 31}{50} = 20.46$$

The expected frequency for 'males, over £25k' is 12.54, and for the two female groups, respectively 10.54 and 6.46.

The formula for chi-square therefore gives:

$$\chi^2 = \frac{(18-20.46)^2}{20.46} + \frac{(15-12.54)^2}{12.54} + \frac{(13-10.54)^2}{10.54} + \frac{(4-6.46)^2}{6.46}$$

$$= 0.30 + 0.48 + 0.57 + 0.94 = 2.29$$

The value of χ^2 required for significance at the 0.05 level with a 2×2 contingency table is 3.84; the value obtained above does not reach this level of significance.

The chi-square test can be used with much larger contingency tables than the one above, although the value of χ^2 required to reach statistical significance increases with the number of cells in the matrix. There are also limitations in the use of the chi-square test: no more than 20% of cells should have expected frequencies of less than 5 and none of them should contain expected frequencies less than one. People wishing to use the chi-square test in practice are therefore encouraged to consult either Maxwell (1970) or Siegel (1956) for further details of use and limitations. Both of these books contain appendices which give the required value of χ^2 for different levels of significance under various conditions.

Levels of significance

In the preceding section we introduced the term 'significance', and earlier in the chapter we discussed the idea of error and accuracy. The technical and common sense versions of these terms are somewhat different. The idea of significance comes from sampling theory. It indicates the probability that, if a sample of the given size was drawn *at random* from a large population, an outcome of that level (size of correlation, chi-square etc) would have been obtained. Conversely the accuracy or confidence level indicates the likelihood, as a percentage, that the observed result could *not* have arisen by chance. When conducting a survey with a genuine sample drawn from a population the confidence level indicates the likelihood that the true attributes of the population lie close to those identified in the sample. When used in this way, the statistics are sometimes known as *inferential statistics*.

However, in many cases significance tests are used on data where there is no population, as such, from which sampling takes place. The test is thus used by the researcher to indicate which outcomes might be important or meaningful. However, any results that show relationships should be examined carefully before claiming causality, because there are many ways that spurious associations can be produced. Maxwell (1970) gives a number of examples of spurious correlations, and Huff (1973) gives a delightful account of how statistics can be used to mislead people.

Statistical packages

Although statistical analysis by hand may give the researcher a 'feel' for the data under consideration, the availability of cheap computer power means that most quantitative analysis is now done with computer packages. These are available in both mainframe and micro-computer formats. It is probably better to use a package that has been available on mainframe for some time since the chances are that many of the bugs will have been sorted out. Two well known packages that meet this criterion are SPSSX (the mainframe version) or SPSS PC+ (the micro-computer version), and MINITAB.

SPSS stands for Statistical Package for the Social Sciences. It is widely used and offers a full range of contemporary statistical methods, plus good editing and labelling facilities. The PC version has an interactive system of menus and an excellent on-line help system. It also has the ability to produce output in both report and table formats, which is very useful for management researchers, and one of the most reassuring aspects of SPSS is the ease with which it handles missing data. However, it is not without disadvantages:

it is expensive to purchase and has a difficult syntax that takes some perseverance to learn. The PC version, SPSS PC+, comes in modular format and thus requires varying amounts of memory dependent on which options are loaded.

MINITAB as a program is friendly, fully interactive and easy to use. Because of these features it is often used for teaching statistics and, as a consequence, students can learn to use the software quickly. For a text on the use of MINITAB see Ryan, Joiner and Ryan (1985). The disadvantages are its limitations in the area of editing and labelling. These are quite important for survey work and, if large surveys are embarked upon, SPSS, once mastered, might well prove the more useful package. (See Norusis, 1986, for more details.)

With the increased use of PCs a whole range of statistical packages for the micro-computer have come onto the market, although SPSS PC+ has in recent years dominated social science PC computing. There are others, such as BMDP, SAS and Systat, which are now almost as popular as SPSS. Systat (version 3) runs on all major PC operating systems (CP/M, MS-DOS, UNIX, Macintosh and VAX) and like SPSS PC+ can be run either interactively or in 'batch' mode. It also provides relatively good on-line help and reads ASCII files. Systat has proved to be one of the most accurate of all statistical packages.

There are also a great range of other packages available for the PC, including statgraphics, Stata and Statpac Gold. In France, STAT/ITCF and SPHINX are widely used. SPHINX is interesting as it incorporates a 'toolbox' and 'expert system' that assists students not only to design their questionnaire, but also to determine the sample size they will need in order to draw significant conclusions from their data. This type of facility helps students to focus on the statistical aspects of data analysis. Because of the number of statistics packages available we have compiled a checklist of questions that researchers might consider before choosing a PC package. In compiling this list we have relied heavily on the advice of Philip Schrudt (1987).

The best advice we can offer in evaluating statistical packages is to check out carefully the facilities and find out just what the package will, and will not, do. Perhaps the simplest way to do this is to ask someone who uses the packages to assist you in the evaluation. Below are some of the questions that might provide helpful pointers to areas of potential concern.

1 How much memory does the program require? For example, SPSS PC+ with all the options loaded except the mapping

module requires a huge 12 Mb.

2 Check the size of data set the program will load, so that it is clear how many cases the program will handle and how many variables per case. An additional point here is to find out what will happen if the program runs out of space. Will the whole program crash, or is there the facility to delete unnecessary data?

3 How fast will the package run? Programs and routines differ greatly in the amount of time they require. Loading from and saving to disks can also take a good deal of time.

4 How friendly are the manuals? Some programs, for example SPSS PC+, come with excellent documentation, but other programs are not nearly so friendly.

5 How well does the program deal with missing data?

6 Can the program read and write ASCII text files so that the facility exists for data to be transferred between machines and downloaded into different programs?

7 How well will the program handle cross-tabulation? Because of the complexity of the non-parametric routines a large amount of memory is often required for cross-tabulations. If problems are going to occur, it is likely that they will begin to surface here.

8 What extra facilities does the program offer for data output, reports, graphics and so on?

9 What is the nature of the program's command structure? Menu-driven programs may appear easy for beginners but there can be problems. On many occasions it may be an advantage to be able to string commands together so that the computer can be left to churn through the analysis without the researcher being in continual attendance.

Mixing methods

Up to this point the discussion in Chapters 5 and 6 has been primarily about the use, and choice, of individual methods of data collection and analysis. However, there are good reasons for using several different methods in the same study. Abrahamson (1983) points out that this approach prevents the research becoming method-bound: the strength of almost every measure is flawed in some way or other, and therefore research designs and strategies can be offset by counterbalancing strengths from one to another.

The use of multiple, but independent, measures is known as *triangulation*, a term borrowed from navigation and surveying where a minimum of three reference points are taken to check an object's location (Smith, 1975). There are four categories, theoretical, data, investigator and methodological triangulation.

Triangulation of theories involves borrowing models from one discipline and using them to explain situations in another discipline. This can frequently reveal insights into data which had previously appeared not to have much importance.

Data triangulation refers to research where data is collected over different time frames or from different sources. Many cross-sectional designs adopt this type of research.

Triangulation by investigators is where different people collect data on the same situation, and the results are then compared. This is one of the advantages of a multi-disciplinary research team as it provides the opportunity for researchers to examine the same situation and to compare, develop and refine themes using insights gained from different perspectives.

Todd (1979) advocates *methodological triangulation*. In his research he used both quantitative as well as qualitative methods of data collection. These were extremely diverse and included questionnaires, interviews, telephone surveys and field studies. He points out that triangulation is not an end in itself, but an imaginative way of maximising the amount of data collected.

This returns us to the discussion in Chapter 3 about the advisability of combining quantitative and qualitative methods. At the philosophical level there is definitely a problem: the positivist perspective which seeks for a single, objective and stable truth is not compatible with the social constructionist view of reality being flexible, fluid and continually renegotiated. Quantitative methods can be used to study both 'hard facts' and human perceptions; likewise qualitative methods can be used and analysed in either objectivist or constructionist ways. Our advice to the researcher is to use different methods from within the same paradigm whenever possible, and also to move across paradigms occasionally, but with care.

7

Finishing Research

Woody Allen, the American comedian and author, has remarked that 90% of the success in writing depends on getting started and finished on time, and the bit in the middle is easy. It seems that this principle applies to the whole process of research, just as much as to the writing phase. Most people thoroughly enjoy gathering data and doing fieldwork; and there is often a strong temptation to continue collecting data for too long because of a basic anxiety that the data will eventually turn out to be inadequate.

This leads to two issues that are considered in this chapter. Firstly, there are the problems of writing, and we consider different styles and strategies that may be adopted to overcome these. Secondly, there is the general anxiety about whether enough work has been done to ensure satisfactory completion of the research project. We therefore review some of the criteria that are likely to be employed in evaluating differing forms of research, and hope this will help the researcher to judge when 'enough is enough'. The chapter concludes with some thoughts about capitalising on the research through publications and other forms of dissemination.

Writing up research

The problems of writing vary somewhat according to the style of research that has been adopted. When quantitative methods and a positivist approach are adopted, there are fairly clear conventions regarding the structure of the report. Each section is fairly self-contained and can be written independently as one proceeds. With qualitative methods the stages are less distinct, and although interim notes should have been produced throughout the course of the research, it is often necessary to rewrite the whole thing at the end.

Whatever style is adopted, one is repeatedly confronted with the blank page: this is exhilarating for some people, and intimidating for others. Many different strategies can be adopted to overcome writing blocks. Some people start writing anything in order to get started, and only begin to work out what they are trying to say once they have written a couple of paragraphs of nonsense. Others cannot put pen to paper, or fingers to keyboard, until they have worked out precisely what they wanted to say. Steinbeck (1970) adopted an interesting strategy when writing *East of Eden* which is mid-way between these two positions. He always began his daily sessions by writing a letter to his editor about what he planned to say that day. The letters were written on the left hand pages of a large note book (and not sent); on the right hand pages he wrote the text of the book. He found this a useful way of starting his thought processes, and overcoming his own writing block.

Becker (1986) takes a slightly different line on how to overcome the barriers to effective writing. He feels that one of the reasons why writing is so difficult is the fear of exposing oneself in public to possible humiliation and ridicule (a thought that has occasionally crossed our minds while writing this book). To overcome this he suggests a six-stage strategy: write with authority; use a direct style of English; be prepared to carry out editing at several stages; be professional and make writing a normal everyday occurrence; confront yourself with the risks of writing by inviting others to read preliminary drafts; and keep to deadlines however difficult it may seem.

Another strategy which we adopted was to draw a 'mind map' of the context of the research. This enabled us to clarify the principal issues which eventually formed chapter 4 of this book. This mind map is set out in Figure 7.1. Many inexperienced researchers worry about how they will communicate their ideas in a formal written format to a critical audience. But they would do well not to emulate the obscure and stilted language which often creeps into academic reports and which has been rightly criticised by Mills (1959) as follows: 'Lack of intelligibility [in scholarly writing], I believe, usually has little or nothing at all to do with the profundity of thought. It has almost entirely to do with certain confusions of the academic writer about his own status' (p. 218).

To increase the chances of the reader understanding what has been written, simplicity should be the main aim. This can be produced not only by avoiding jargon and complicated sentence construction, but also by using an *active* rather than passive style of writing. In other words, use concrete examples wherever possible instead of abstract concepts. Amplify ideas by adopting easily understood examples on all possible occasions. Use *metaphors* to give greater depth to the meaning and interpretation of ideas and theories.

Presenting qualitative research
One of the most difficult problems to overcome in dealing with qualitative data is how to communicate, in a systematic and honest

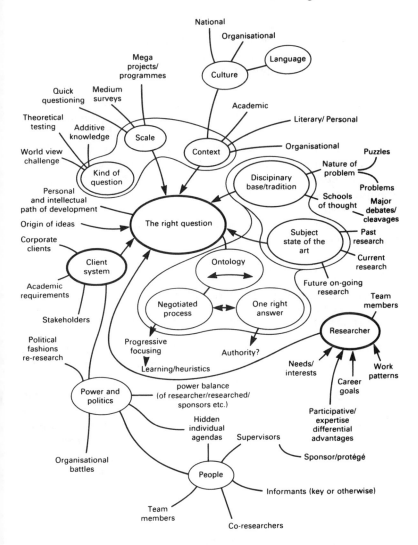

Figure 7.1 *Mind map of the context of research – getting the right question: a mind map developed for this book*

manner, research findings to a readership who may not be very familiar with the detailed context of the research. Journalists are paid to interpret situations in a manner which is of interest to their readers, and this often requires editing out issues that they believe will not be of interest. Researchers will also need to edit their findings, but there is a difference here. One never finds out what the journalist has excluded, but the researcher has a duty not only to demonstrate what the line of argument is, but also to indicate what information supports *and* opposes this argument.

Fineman and Mangham (1983) in a persuasive article on qualitative data suggest that in their experience it has been the 'soft' qualitative parts that have saved many of the research studies of the day, not the 'hard' quantitative parts. Whereas qualitative data can be both 'rich' and 'deep', quantitative data which is obtained at a distance from everyday activities may have ceased to 'live'. What Fineman and Mangham suggest qualitative researchers need to do, therefore, is to convey the richness of their experience. For example, consider this short extract from research by Nichols (1980) drawn from a miner's diary, discussing the influence of a monetary incentive scheme on the miner's willingness to work at higher levels of performance.

> All the time we were packing unnecessarily, the coal was going, so no time could be booked, plus the fact that me and my two were working on dangerous uncovered ground. I was seriously injured a few years ago and this was in the back of my mind. I was off work on crutches for 8 months and all the bonus in the world is not worth being injured for again.

Left like this the passage is understandable to all. But qualitative researchers need to take it further by developing theoretical themes and highlighting patterns grounded in the data in a way that can be recognised by an external body. This element of presenting findings for others to criticise is an important feature of all types of research. To be regarded as valid, research needs to have been placed in the public domain so that it can be debated and defended.

Other ways of ensuring validity in qualitative research are:

1 Feed back the conclusions to the subjects (co-researchers) for verification.
2 Spell out the nature of the relationships, and the settings in which the observations and discussions took place; also state the degree of collaboration involved.
3 Ensure that honesty and values take a high place on the agenda of any research work undertaken. Honesty about the limitations of the research will increase confidence in the positive results that are presented.
4 Spell out the standpoint you are taking. Reference frames from past experiences are bound to bias you in one way or another, and they are bound to creep into qualitative research. These should not be ignored but declared and, where appropriate, explained.

Presenting quantitative research

As we have suggested above there are more definite conventions when presenting quantitative research: in order to reflect the assumed objectivity of the researcher the writing style tends to be more formal and distanced. Whereas the qualitative researcher should write in the first person whenever possible, this practice is still frowned upon by quantitative researchers.

There is also a standard format to the research report which goes along the following lines (Nisbet and Entwistle, 1984):

1 outline of the research
2 review of previous work
3 statement of scope, aims and hypotheses
4 description of procedures, samples and methods used
5 statement of results
6 discussion
7 summary and conclusions
8 list of references.

The report can be enlivened by graphical presentation of descriptive statistics, often in glorious technicolour. Unfortunately some researchers seem to become fascinated by the potential of colour graphics, and forget about the messages they are intended to convey. Beware, large numbers of beautiful pie charts and histograms in a project report are often a sign that limited thought has been given to the conclusions.

Some practical tips

We have emphasised the importance of getting started, anyhow, and the need to adopt different strategies according to the individual's preferences. One of the key points in writing is to adopt a medium which causes the least obstruction between one's head and the paper or screen. Mark sometimes writes on paper, sometimes on a word processor, and sometimes it all tumbles out onto an audio tape. The same session may start in one mode, switch to another, and then another. Having a good place to write also helps. Many academics claim to have written their key books while on sabbatical in Tuscany or the South of France. To provide the right frame of mind it is important to establish the association between a place and the ability to work. Other aspects of ritual may also be important: a room, the time of day, the correct type of paper, or one's favourite biro.

Finally, when writing it is most important not to feel constrained by what has been written. It is often necessary to write several drafts before getting a document right. Each draft should be discarded not with regret, but as part of development and improvement. Ideally, successive drafts should get shorter, rather than longer. Those wishing to read more about the art of writing could consult some of the following works which we have found helpful: Barzun and Graff (1977) or Becker (1986).

Evaluative criteria

Part of the problem in finishing research is in knowing when one has done sufficient to meet the success criteria that are likely to be applied. These vary considerably from one piece to another. We discuss here the criteria that may be applied in evaluating four common forms of research activity.

Dissertations for Masters' courses are the commonest form of research project in the management field. These normally include some theoretical ideas, based on literature and some form of data collected by the researcher. The general quality of the dissertation will depend on how well the overall theme/argument is maintained and the extent to which theory and data can be synthesised. It is not sufficient to provide either a good description of others' work or a good account of data gathered; it is important to go beyond what is immediately presented by providing some form of critical reflection. Bloom's taxonomy of educational objectives (Bloom and Krathwohl, 1956) provides a useful framework for thinking about the academic quality of a piece of work. There are six levels of hierarchy, as follows:

6 Evaluation
5 Synthesis
4 Analysis
3 Application
2 Comprehension
1 Knowledge

There is some debate at the moment about whether it is more important for management dissertations to demonstrate evidence of 'application' or 'analysis', and this derives from a long-standing debate in the UK about whether management education should be a practical or an academic training (Whitley et al., 1981). Whatever one's view on this, one should be aware that Master's degrees are awarded by academics and it is therefore prudent to include some elements of analysis and synthesis in work submitted.

Doctoral theses are similar to Masters' dissertations in that they require a synthesis of ideas and data. But they need to go further in providing critical evaluation of relevant work, and demonstrating some kind of original contribution to the field. This contribution can be provided in three main forms: as new knowledge about the world of management, as new theories and ideas, or as new methods of investigation. Ideally the thesis should contain some element of each, although one form may be dominant.

An element of consistency is important in a thesis; it should contain one, or more, clear arguments which are supported by evidence presented in the document. The title of a thesis is also very important because it gives a hint of the degree of clarity and focus that is likely to ensue in the rest of the document. Beyond that, the degree of emphasis on, say, the accuracy of methodology or the creativity of ideas produced depends on the philosophical base underlying the research. Since the final evaluation is conducted by an independent external examiner it is most important that the examiner is sympathetic to the world view, or paradigm, of the researcher. This is not a matter of 'rigging' the result, but of ensuring that one gets a fair hearing.

Research projects supported by academic Research Councils invoke slightly different criteria. While the conduct of the research must be carried out with the same rigour as a doctoral degree (and be available for public scrutiny), the project will also be conducted within the framework of the proposal for which funds were awarded.

There are three points to note here, perhaps in descending order of importance. Firstly, the project report must demonstrate that the research has achieved the objectives defined in the original proposal, and that any hypotheses have been tested, whether results are positive, negative or ambiguous. Any departure from the original objectives must be clearly explained and justified. Secondly, it is important to show that the amount of data collected, and the overall effort put into the project, were as originally specified. And thirdly, it is worth showing that the outcomes from the project justify the financial expenditure incurred.

Consultancy projects involve work funded and carried out for clients where there is often a strong emphasis on application or action research. In these cases there is usually some flexibility with regard to the achievement of objectives – these can often be renegotiated with the client. The crucial elements are clarity and brevity of the conclusions and recommendations. Explanation of methods and theoretical implications requires very limited treatment: much of this will be taken for granted by the client. Consultancy reports are often used by clients, and other managers, as a justification for change or for getting their own way. As such, it is most important in these cases to be sensitive to the political aspects of research discussed in Chapter 4.

A common problem is where a consultancy project is also used as the vehicle for obtaining a Master's degree, because the expectations and criteria of the industrial client and academic assessors may be quite different. It may still be possible to produce a report for a client which has sufficient elements of reflection and critical thought. If not, then the consultancy report can be sandwiched within a more academic commentary which reflects on choices made, evaluates experiences, and develops any theoretical insights that might be relevant.

Capitalising on the research

In Chapter 2 we used the story of Fleming's discovery of penicillin as an illustration of some of the factors that underlie scientific discoveries. There is a sequel to that story which relates to capitalising on research.

Fleming discovered penicillin in 1923, but after undertaking only one experiment when he injected penicillin into a mouse and found that it disappeared from the blood stream within 30 minutes, he concluded that it would have little therapeutic application. Ten years later, Howard Florey and Ernest Chain, working with a team at Oxford, uncovered Fleming's description of penicillin following a systematic review of the literature (Macfarlane, 1985). Although the paper ignored previous literature on bacteriological inhibition and was vague about the chemical properties, it did note that the therapeutic potential might be worthy of further investigation. Florey and Chain concentrated on penicillin and eventually produced sufficient quantities to be able to demonstrate its life-saving properties. The results were published in a leading article in *The Times*. Following this, Sir Almroth Wright, the head of Fleming's department, saw an opportunity to increase charitable contributions to St Mary's, and wrote a letter to the Editor claiming credit for penicillin for Fleming. The upshot was that Fleming was given the major credit in the form of 25 honorary degrees, 15 civic freedoms and 140 honours, despite the fact that he had conducted no further research on the topic during the eleven years following his experiment with the mouse.

The lesson from this story is that credit for research should not be taken for granted; it depends very much on how much the researcher is able to exploit his work through contacts, publications and other forms of dissemination.

The best route depends somewhat on the kind of research undertaken. With Masters' projects the pay-off might be quite direct, since they are often used as a demonstration of practical competence or relevant experience by those who are looking for jobs. Even consultancy projects can be written up in journals aimed at practitioners. If the journal has a large circulation, like *Management Today* or *Training and Development*, publication of past projects will lead to an enhanced reputation, if not directly to further consultancy opportunities. The best way of getting into practitioner journals is to note carefully the house style, and remember that the article will need to appeal to a fairly broad readership. Straight description of the project is unacceptable; articles need to be able to raise issues and answer questions that readers are likely to be interested in – the project results can then be incorporated to illustrate wider issues.

With academic research projects and theses the natural outlets are refereed journals, and these are very important for people seeking to make academic careers. In most cases academic journals look for articles with a narrow focus and well supported argument; economy of style and expression are less important than with practitioner journals. In theory, publication decisions depend on the comments of anonymous referees who are unaware of the author's identity. In practice the editor(s) often have to make decisions amid conflicting advice from referees, and anonymity is not always maintained because referees who are very expert in a particular field may well be able to identify the contributions of different authors. The editors of most refereed journals try to be as fair as possible, without showing undue bias towards friends and colleagues. But, all things being equal, it still seems to help if one is known to the editor.

That is why it is important for the aspiring academic to go to conferences in order to develop the kind of networks that we discussed in Chapter 4. It is also worth offering to present research findings and ideas at these conferences. At best one might be spotted by an editor or academic dean as a new and rising talent. At the very least one is likely to get some critical feedback on the paper which can be used to strengthen its claim to future publication.

Finally there is the possibility of publishing a book. Not many management theses, as such, find their way into book form. This is because a good thesis is likely to be far too narrow and focused to be of interest to more than a handful of readers. A few publishers are still prepared to accept academic work; but decisions are increasingly driven by commercial considerations, and books are not likely to be accepted unless a sizable market can be clearly defined for the topic.

Peters and Waterman (1982) are reputed to have received royalties of $1.8M in the first year of their book's publication, and Mintzberg (1973) did well out of his book (unusually, based on his PhD thesis). But these are the exception: for most people the direct financial rewards are not great. Fortune is most likely to follow the fame of being a published author, and academic careers depend on both the reputation of the publisher and the quality of the reviews that ensue. The nice thing about books is that it is usually possible to develop ideas over a period of time with the help of the publisher's editor. Once again contacts with publishers are most easily established at conferences, where most of the relevant houses are represented.

As with all forms of publishing it is important to believe that one has something worth saying. Taking it further, we see publication and dissemination of ideas not merely as a means to the researcher's own ends but as an obligation that each researcher should accept as soon as he or she embarks on research. We hope that this book will have provided some of the armoury both to complete worthwhile research, and to use it.

Appendix: Searching the Management Literature

Researchers undertaking projects, whether theses, dissertations, or funded by outside agencies, need to display a knowledge of the literature in their chosen field.

A library for all intents and purposes is the simplest of systems to operate. But most readers who have experience of them may agree that using a library can give rise to frustration, when books are never on the shelves, or vital articles are delayed. Some even believe that being in the actual building 'blunts the inquiring mind' or that 'libraries send everyone to sleep'. But whatever your impressions, make no mistake, behind the library shelves, keeping on top of an ever increasing quantity of information (10,000 publishing outlets in Great Britain – 125,000 items in print in the area of social sciences alone – 8,000 available journals and 5 million entries in the catalogue of the British Museum, a library that makes the best possible attempt to list all published items), work some highly trained and professional information scientists.

The single most important aspect of using a library is to establish a rapport with one or a number of these professionals and, once the contact has been established, never to let it lapse. The ability to do this effectively means that the researcher has a 'go-between' – someone who can communicate with the library system on his behalf. This is particularly important, as undertaking research can require a higher level of speciality in library use than is normally required.

We assume familiarity with the general arrangements in libraries and knowledge of how to use the three parts of the catalogue commonly found in Britain, that is, the author catalogue, the subject index and the classified catalogue. For those not familiar with these, most libraries now have on-line computer catalogues with good facilities.

Our aim is to indicate how you might set about reviewing the literature from two perspectives: firstly, when you need to gain a comprehensive overview of the literature in a particular field, and secondly, when you know exactly what items of the literature you require and just need to collect them. To distinguish between these two aims, we have borrowed terminology from Selvin and Stuart (1966) and called the former 'trawling' and the second 'fishing'.

'Trawling'

Before entering the library on a trawl to see what you can catch, you can save time by reviewing exactly what you require. More specifically, there is a need to think about the words you use in identifying your subject area.

An example might be GAS DISTRIBUTION. In Britain this might refer to North Sea gas, and in an American database it would refer to petrol. Then again, are you looking at its distribution by piping from a field to shore or the conveyance of gas under pressure by lorry? The subject heading GAS DISTRIBUTION may just as easily relate to areas outside industry, such as physical geography or civil engineering.

The point we are making is that terminology is very important: to find what you want from the mass of information in the library it is important to identify your interests clearly.

A subject-search demands as a precondition keywords identifying your subject. Don't think that you have to find an exact match with the words used by the library to name a subject – any classification system provides for alternative 'names' and your part is to be aware of the most likely alternatives. Start by writing a list of the different ways your subject area might be described.

We realise that you haven't entered the library yet and you might already be entering one of those periods of frustration, so let us underline three of the pitfalls you might encounter.

Firstly, don't be afraid to change your concept of what you're looking for. If you knew everything there is to know about your subject you wouldn't be involved in this sort of research. For example, returning to GAS DISTRIBUTION – the wrong keywords can give some crazy titles, like 'The Cellular Structure of Air Balloons in the 21st Century'. Keywords clearly work better in some fields than others, but mistaken terminology can sometimes help to refine your objectives. If your search reveals many works on the economics of tanker delivery or the civil engineering aspects of pipelining, then your conception of what is included in your subject expands.

Secondly, don't be misled into thinking that an excessively detailed analysis of the subject area shortcuts research – that is, unless you find someone has already undertaken exactly the study you intend.

Research as we have discussed it is not about refining what others have said, it is in part an act of synthesis. In this case it involves industrial psychology (fatigue – separation), management (timetabling – rostering) and the North Sea oil industry. Detailed analysis of your subject will provide keywords for you to commence your search but it won't do it for you.

Thirdly, don't expect a single document match. For example, a string of summarising keywords, such as FATIGUE – MARRIED MEN (See also separation: psychology) – IN THE OIL INDUSTRY – NORTH SEA PLATFORMS: (Significance for) WORK ROSTERS, is unlikely to throw up a specific work on the subject.

At long last, you can enter the library. As we have discussed in our examples the literature on management comprises a wide range of subjects and is continually expanding, but fortunately there are a number of bibliographical publications and document services which can assist in the searches.

Both the literature and the bibliographical publications which are the key to information searching fall roughly into five broad groupings:

1 Books
2 Periodicals
3 Theses and research in progress
4 Government publications and official statistics
5 Reference works, general guides to the literature, and guides to the literature in particular subject areas.

A good strategy is to begin by fully exploiting the publications in your own library; if necessary, the search can then be carried further by means of the inter-library loan system (which takes some time).

Remember, too, that the extent of your search will also be bounded by how far back you wish to go and the subject headings used in the bibliographies and abstracting indexes. If material is not being found, broader headings can be used (remember for example that Americans call companies corporations) and, if the material needs to be more specific to reduce the volume, a thesaurus of management indexing terms and one of a number of dictionaries on management might be useful.

Books

Most libraries arrange their books by subject according to the Dewey Decimal system of classification. There may be some modification to suit local requirements. Browsing amongst books in your subject area can be useful, but will always provide a partial and unrevealing picture of your subject area. If all aspects of an example of North Sea oil were grouped in one place, literature searching would be relatively simple, but there is a scatter of subjects from geology through marine engineering, economics, industrial sociology, psychology, management, energy, ecology. The list isn't endless but its logic arises from the general structure of knowledge, which is far from immediately obvious.

The catalogue is, therefore, the best place for a researcher to start a search for books, but if the subject is a fairly specific one there may not be many books on it, and there may be a need to look under a wider heading in the subject index. It is likely that there will be several entries, using our example, on the North Sea oil industry in general, or more specifically on fatigue at work. Some of these might contain bibliographies (that is, lists of references to books and journal articles) that point the way to other potentially useful items.

A subject index and catalogue can also reveal any relevant bibliographies in the library's stock.

If it is obvious at this stage that there are other published bibliographies which are relevant to the research then the next step is to consult one of the guides that list bibliographies. The *Bibliographic Index* is a list of both separately published bibliographies and those occurring in books and articles. By examining this, it should be possible to find references to promising bibliographies, including books that are in the stock of the library.

The output of published material has become so great that it is unlikely that any library will be able to meet all of a researcher's needs from its own resources, so once the stock of books available in the local library has been reviewed the researcher may want to take things further and see what else has been written. To do this appropriate national bibliographies need to be consulted. These list the book output of individual countries. The main bibliographies in the English language are the *British National Bibliography* (blue volumes) and the American *Cumulative Book Index* (large brown volumes).

The entries in the *British National Bibliography* are arranged in a classified subject order (in fact, it is arranged according to the Dewey Decimal Classification), and the weekly parts are eventually cumulated into annual volumes. There is a need to check the subject index at the back of the most recent annual volume and then turn to the entries at the appropriate classification number. 658.3 for example is the 'Personnel' number, but care needs to be exercised because, just as when browsing on the shelves under the appropriate classification number, who is to say that certain elements of industrial relations (331.0) and industrial sociology (306.3), factory law (344.01) and economics (330), don't have a bearing on the aspect of personnel management that interests you? Searching in the subject index under one or more headings might also reveal entries in the cumulation for a given period.

The *Cumulative Book Index* is in many ways easier to use, being arranged alphabetically, with entries under subject keywords, authors and titles. If the research has an international flavour, as North Sea oil does, then it will almost certainly be worthwhile consulting other national bibliographies, such as the French *Biblio* now superseded by *LIVRES-HEBDO 1979–*, the German *Deutsche Bibliographie*, and the Spanish *Bibliografía Española*. To do this effectively you need at the very least to know the foreign equivalents of the subject keywords under which you are searching, but it is obviously preferable to have a more extensive knowledge of the foreign language concerned or access to an interpreter. For the non-linguist there are sources of information about works that have been translated, such as the *Index Translationum* and the British Lending Library's *BLLD Announcement Bulletin*; the Association of Special Libraries and Information Bureaux also compiles an *Index to Unpublished Translations*.

Before finally leaving books, it is worth remembering that printed, book-form catalogues of other libraries can also be a very useful source. The printed catalogues are, of course, restricted to the holdings of the library concerned, but are not limited to the output of any particular country. In the case of great libraries, such as the *British Museum* or the *Library of Congress*, the point about restriction of holdings is a bit academic, since their intake of material is so vast that they can be said to hold most English-language material and a good, though declining, proportion of foreign-language publications. Examples of more specific printed catalogues are those of the Library of the Institute of Chartered Accountants, which goes under the name of *Current Accounting Literature*, and the *Core Collection – an Author and Subject Guide* of the Baker Library at the Harvard Business School.

Periodicals

For most research purposes a library's principal resource is its *periodicals* collection. There are a number of ways in which articles might be found which are relevant to specific interests. For example, you could leaf through some of the best-known business journals, or you could identify the journals dealing with your particular subject area and scan them by means of their annual indexes. However, a much more effective way of locating articles of interest is to use the appropriate abstracting and indexing services, since by doing this you can scan as many as several hundred journals at a time, and come across articles in journals you might never have thought of. An abstracting service not only provides you with references to journal articles but also includes an abstract of the subject matter; an index, on the other hand, simply gives full bibliographical details of references.

For example, in the *British Humanities Index* for 1985:

Johnson Matthey Bank
Banks will continue to go bust – the need is to spot it happening earlier. Hamish McRae *Guardian* (22 June 1985) P20.

An abstracting service example in *'the compleat'* Anbar No 15:

Metal Box
T Jackson on the management page of **The Financial Times** (UK), 23 May 86 –
In talking with Brian Smith, the new head of packaging group Metal Box, looks at the Company's aims to be more sensitive to the market, eg in its use of its research establishment ('research is too important a resource to be left to the researchers'), and its joint venture with Alcoa in the US, having sold its own factory in the States. Dwells greatly on Mr Smith's previous experiences with ICI.

Most business school libraries and many universities and polytechnics have a good selection of the abstracts and indexes which cover the subject areas of interest to management. The two most useful general services are Britain's *Anbar Abstracts*, which are arranged in six subject groups with an alphabetical 'keyword register' as the key to the classification, and the American *Business Periodicals Index*, which, as its name suggests, is purely an indexing service.

Anbar is probably the most accessible of all the indexes. It contains sections on: accounting and data processing, top management, personnel and training, marketing and distribution, management services and production and, most recently, information management and technology abstracts. You should first look to the 'keyword register', which will then refer you to the appropriate numbered code in the *Index* for the various subject headings. The abstracts of these can then be looked up to see if they do indeed throw light on the issue under research. Anbar is considered by some to be a little cumbersome; the *Business Periodicals Index* is a good deal simpler. Here you need to search for references under the subject heading required. The index then offers 'see also' references to look under different headings. Note that a reference to a particular article can of course occur under several different subject headings in an alphabetically arranged indexing service of this kind.

Another general service that can be particularly useful for tracing up-to-date information is the *Research Index*. This is primarily concerned with financial, economic and company information, and scans the national press and some relevant journals. This service appears every fortnight with quarterly cumulations, and includes items which were published from 1 to 3 weeks previously, which is about as up to date as you can get with this type of service.

In addition to general abstracts and indexes, there are a number which deal with more specific subject areas, for example, *Personnel Management Abstracts*, *International Abstracts in Operations Research*, *Marketing Information Guide*, *Packaging Abstracts*, *Psychological Abstracts*, *Training Abstracts* – and many more, including some, such as the *Public Affairs Information Service Bulletin* and the *British Technology Index* which, whilst not central to management studies, may be useful. One abstracting service we have found useful is the Work Research Unit's Abstracts that appear quarterly. This is published by the Department of Employment and is sent at no charge providing you are on their mailing list. The publication also includes the reports of conferences and notification of future conferences in the area of management. In fact it is likely that there is an abstracting or indexing service that covers whatever you want.

Most abstracts and indexes are published monthly, but there is usually a time-lag of several months between an article's publication and its appearance in these services so, if you require really up-to-date references you will need to get them by means of what are known as current awareness services. These usually consist of reproductions of the contents pages of recent issues of journals, and are purely alerting services, with no cumulations or indexes. The Department of Trade and Industry's *Contents of Recent Economics Journals* (weekly) and *Contents Pages in Management* (fortnightly), put out by the Manchester Business School Library, are examples of current awareness services. In addition, many libraries prepare their own 'home-made' current awareness services specially tailored for local circulation.

The European Index of Management Periodicals covers the main European journals on management and business studies and the more important American journals.

Theses and research in progress

Another important area which you have to consider is that of theses and research in progress. One of the most comprehensive and up-to-date listings of theses is *Dissertation Abstracts International*, which is sub-divided into Section A: Humanities and Social Sciences, Section B: Physical Sciences and Engineering, and Section C: European Abstracts. *Dissertation Abstracts* includes most theses produced in North America, and copies can be borrowed from the British Library Document Supply Centre (BLDSC) at Boston Spa. Section A is probably the one most management students need to consult, but if your subject concerns computers, mathematics, statistics or operational research, you will also need to have a look at Section B; both sections have a cumulative index for volumes 1–29. The index is in nine volumes, and volume 8 is the one that includes business subjects. A check needs to be made under keywords. If there is no thesis listed which is of interest, then you will need to check the individual volumes following the compilation of the cumulative index. If no theses are found, it should not be considered a waste of time since it is helping to ensure that there is no duplication of research. As the cost of duplicated research is very high, searches of this kind can be a very worthwhile exercise.

The British counterpart of *Dissertation Abstracts* is the *Aslib Index to Theses with Abstracts accepted for Higher Degrees by the Universities of Great Britain and Ireland and the Council of National Academic Awards*. It is not so up to date as the American service, but attempts are being made to improve its currency and to make British theses more readily available via the British Library Document Supply Centre. Other countries have similar lists, and you could usefully consult France's *Catalogue des Thèses et Ecrits Académiques* and Germany's *Jahresverzeichnis der Deutschen Hochschulschriften*.

Information on research actually in progress is not easy to come by, and it is here that experienced researchers, who tend to build up a network of contacts over the years, have a considerable advantage. However, the Department of Education and Science's annual publication, *Scientific Research in British Universities and Colleges*, is an important source, as is the Economic and Social Science Research Council's newsletter, *ESRC Newsletter*, which publishes headings including 'management'; and *Graduate Management Research*, a small journal published by Cranfield Institute in conjunction with a number of other universities. This journal provides an opportunity for Masters' and PhD research students to discuss aspects of their research. Other possible sources of information include the registers of current research published by several leading business schools.

Government publications, official statistics
The government, through the Stationery Office, publishes a vast

number of reports and statistical series, many of which are of importance to management researchers. In some libraries government publications are not catalogued or classified and are therefore kept in a separate section. However, it is likely that in most academic libraries they will be classified and traceable by means of the catalogue.

In order to trace British government publications, a researcher should refer to the annual *List of Government Publications* or, if necessary, to the *Monthly* and *Daily* lists. This involves first looking at the index at the back of each annual *List* for headings that appear to be of interest or 'fit' the keywords that describe the subject. There are a number of published introductions to British government publications and official statistics, and many libraries produce their own guides to their stock of official publications. A look through one or more of these can be very useful. For more comprehensive information on what official statistics are available, the Central Statistical Office's *Guide to Official Statistics* is an invaluable source. However, the whole area of British government publications and, in particular, the maze of official statistics present problems to the uninitiated, so here is an occasion when the friendly librarian becomes invaluable.

The publications of foreign governments and of international organisations are usually catalogued and classified in the normal way. It is also useful to consult the annual HMSO Agency Catalogue. This is very useful for tracking down publications of, for example, the OECD or the United Nations which may not be held in the library.

Reference works, general guides to the literature and
guides to the literature in particular subject areas
The final group of publications that a researcher needs to know something about is that of reference works, general guides to the literature, and guides to specific subject areas. New researchers can use reference works, for example, to become aware of any organisations that are relevant to their interests, since these are often very fertile sources of information, and are usually willing to help outside inquirers.

If you want to find out what reference works there are relevant to your topic you can consult A.J. Walford's *Guide to Reference Material* and *Current British Directories*, or its counterpart *Current European Directories*.

For information on companies, possible sources include the *Guide to Key British Enterprises*, the *Kompass* series of directories, *Who Owns Whom*, and *The Times 1,000*. Alternatively, if you are seeking more detailed information on a particular company, your local library will probably subscribe to the British and European services of the *Extel Financial Company Card Service*, known as 'Extel cards', which provide detailed, mainly financial, data on all quoted British companies (including unit trusts), and about 300 major European companies. MIRAC also provides up-to-date information on individual companies. Other sources include the *International Stock Exchange Yearbook* and *Mergers and Acquisitions*, a Financial Times monthly journal published by FT Business Information Service. Services such as DATASTREAM and EXSTAT give 'on-line' access to financial data.

Share prices can be viewed on the statistical pages of the *Financial Times* or by using the *Stock Exchange Daily Official List*. For up-to-date press comment on individual companies, the 'Companies' section of *Research Index*, which was mentioned earlier, is a valuable source.

On-line searching
Just one final word on 'trawling'. The advent of new technology has meant that most academic libraries now have the facilities for undertaking 'on-line' literature searches. Most facilities enable a range of national and international databases to be accessed, many specialising in particular subject areas. For management literature these include Management Contents and ABI/Inform.

Although such a facility may appear appealing to the first-time researcher and 'a quick way' of gaining a print-out of the literature in a particular field there are problems.

Firstly, the service can be very expensive for the library undertaking the search on your behalf. Libraries have budgets for on-line searching and won't want to use up this facility on researchers who could adequately gain what they require manually. However, many databases (such as ABI/Inform) are now being produced on CD-ROM. This development can only increase the availability of mechanised searching to more and more library users.

Secondly, on-line searching relies more than any other type of literature searching on having the words that describe your subject area specified extremely carefully. As with all computer systems, 'garbage in' will produce 'garbage out' and it is not uncommon for initial searches to yield hundreds and hundreds of references on a topic, before it can be more closely specified and reduced to manageable numbers of articles that are likely to be of the most assistance in the research.

Thirdly, although on-line searching does at times yield some extremely valuable material, as soon as you go international, the time delay on receiving articles grows, particularly if articles need translating. This might serve only to increase the frustration quotient of impatient researchers, particularly at the beginning of research!

'Fishing'

Our second aspect of literature searching involves the mechanics of how to retrieve a book or article that gets caught in the 'trawl'.

Firstly, write each reference on a separate card or slip of paper to facilitate sorting and re-arrangement, and cite the elements of the references in a consistent order.

Books can be obtained by consulting the Author index. Once the book has been identified, it can be located on the shelves via the classification system the library uses. There are five such systems: UDC, Dewey Decimal, Library of Congress, Bliss and Colon.

If the book is not stocked, then it may be obtained either by visiting another library or by sending off through the inter-library loan system to the British Library Document Supply Centre. The latter can take time, and the former requires either a reciprocal loan agreement, or time to trawl and to sit and read the book in the library.

Articles in journals can be either taken from the shelves and photocopied or, if more than a few months old, retrieved from the bound 'back copies' or microfiches. Again, if not stocked by the library, they can be obtained by inter-library loan, as can completed theses from most British universities or polytechnics.

In connection with getting hold of specific material of relevance, it is important to know something about a bibliographical aid known as 'citation indexing'. Briefly, a citation index brings together all the other papers that have subsequently made reference to a given paper, and is the only indexing method that enables a researcher to search forward in the literature.

This type of indexing is based on the concept that an author's references to previous articles identify much of the earlier work that is relevant to his present paper, and are themselves the best indicators of its subject. The *Science Citation Index* has been available to researchers in the sciences and technologies since 1963. In 1973 the *Social Sciences Citation Index* was launched, with a coverage of 1,000 journals. This was a major development in literature searching for social scientists, as its value increases as the database grows in size with the passage of time. To begin searching for articles on your particular subject in the *Social Sciences Citation Index* you only need to know the name of one author who has written something on or related to your chosen topic; you can then find all the articles up to the present that have cited the earlier article.

Citation indexes are therefore valuable bibliographical aids for those who wish to trace the development of a topic or field.

Note

This appendix has been based on a paper by N.R. Hunter, librarian at Bradford University, who has kindly agreed to the use of his material.

References and Bibliography

Abrahamson, M. (1983) *Social Research Methods*, Englewood Cliffs, NJ: Prentice Hall.

Agar, M.H. (1986) *Speaking of Ethnography*, Beverly Hills: Sage.

Aiken, H.D. (1956) *The Age of Ideology*, New York: Mentor.

Ansoff, I. (1986) 'The Pathology of Applied Research in Social Science' in F. Heller (ed.), *The Use and Abuse of Social Science*, Beverly Hills: Sage.

Argyris, C. and Schon, D.A. (1978) *Organisational Learning*, Reading: Addison-Wesley.

Ashton, D.J.L. and Easterby-Smith, M. (1979) *Management Development in the Organisation*, London: Macmillan.

Austin, J.H. (1978) *Chase, Chance and Creativity*, New York: Columbia University Press.

Bainbridge, W.S. (1989) *Survey Research: A Computer Assisted Introduction*, Belmont, CA: Wasworth.

Bannister, D. and Fransella, F. (1971) *Inquiring Man: The Theory of Personal Constructs*, Harmondsworth: Penguin.

Bannister, D. and Mair, J.M.M. (1968) *The Evaluation of Personal Constructs*, London: Academic Press.

Barwise, P., Marsh, P., Thomas, K. and Wensley, R. (1989) 'Intelligent Elephants and Part-time Researchers', *Graduate Management Research*, Winter; 12–33.

Barzun, J. and Graff, H.F. (1977) *The Modern Researcher*, New York: Harcourt Brace.

Bateson, G. (1973) *Steps to an Ecology of Mind*, London: Paladin.

Becker, H.S. (1958) 'Problems of Inference and Proof of Participant Observation', *American Sociological Review*, 23: 632–60.

Becker, H. (1986) *Writing for Social Scientists*, Chicago: University of Chicago Press.

Beer, S. (1975) *Platform for Change*, Chichester: Wiley.

Belbin, R.M. (1981) *Management Teams: Why they Succeed or Fail*, London: Heinemann.

Bell, J., Bush, T., Fox, A. Goodley, J. and Goulding, S. (1984) (eds), *Conducting Small Scale Investigations in Education Management*, London: Harper & Row.

Berger, P.L. and Luckman, T. (1966) *The Social Construction of Reality*, London: Penguin.

Beynon, H. (1973) *Working for Ford*, Harmondsworth: Penguin.

Beynon, H. (1988) 'Regulating Research: Politics and Decision Making in Industrial Organisations' in A. Bryman (ed.), *Doing Research in Organisations*, London: Routledge.

Billig, M. (1988) 'Review of: *Murderous Science: Elimination by Scientific Selection of Jews, Gypsies and Others. Germany 1933–1945*, B. Muller-Hill, Oxford: OUP', in *The Psychologist*, December 1988: 475–6.

Bloom, B.S. and Krathwohl, D.R. (1956) *Taxonomy of Educational Objectives*, MacKay & Co.

Bocock, R. (1974) *Ritual in Industrial Society*, London: Allen & Unwin.

Bogdan, R. and Taylor, S.J. (1975) *Introduction to Quantitative Research Methods: A Phenomenological Approach to the Social Sciences*, London: Wiley.

Boissevain, J. (1974) *Friends of Friends*, Oxford: Blackwell.

Bott, E. (1971) *The Family and Social Networks*, New York: The Free Press.

Bowey, A.M. and Thorpe, R. with Hellier, P. (1986) *Payment Systems and Productivity*, London: Macmillan.

Boxer, P. (1980) 'Reflective Learning' in J. Beck and C. Cox (ed.) *Advances in Management Education*, Chichester: Wiley.

Brownell, P. and Trotman, K. (1988) 'Research Methods in Behavioural Accounting' in K.R. Ferris (ed.) *Behavioral Accounting Research: A Critical Analysis*, Columbus, Ohio: Century VII.

Bryn, S. (1966): *The Human Perspective in Sociology*, Englewood Cliffs, NJ: Prentice-Hall

Buchanan, D. (1980) 'Gaining Management Skills through Academic Research Work', *Personnel Management*, 12(4): 45–8.

Buchanan, D.A., Boddy, D. and McCalman, J. (1988) 'Getting in, Getting on, Getting out, Getting back: the Art of the Possible', pp. 53–67 in A. Bryman (ed.) *Doing Research in Organisations*, London: Routledge.

Bulmer, M. (1988) 'Some Reflections upon Research in Organisations' in A. Bryman (ed.) *Doing Research in Organisations*, London: Routledge.

Burgess, R.G. (1982) *Field Research: A Source Book and Field Manual*, London: Allen & Unwin.

Burgoyne, J. and Hodgson, V.E. (1983) 'Natural Learning and Managerial Action: a Phenomenological Study in the Field Setting', *Journal of Management Studies*, 20(3): 387–9

Burgoyne, J. and Stuart, R. (1976) 'The Nature, Use and Acquisition of Managerial Skills and Other Attributes', *Personnel Review*, 15(4): 19–29.

Burrell, G. and Morgan, G. (1979) *Sociological Paradigms and Organisational Analysis*, London: Heinemann.

Calder, A. and Sheridan, D. (eds) (1984) *Speak for yourself: a mass-observation anthology 1937–49*, London: Jonathan Cape.

Campbell, D.T. and Fiske, D.W. (1959) 'Covergent and Discriminant Validation by the Multitrait–Multimethod Matrix', *Psychological Bulletin*, 56: 81–105.

Campbell, D.T. and Stanley, J.C. (1963) 'Experimental and Quasi-Experimental Designs for Research' in N.L. Gage (ed.) *Handbook of Research on Teaching*, Chicago: Rand McNally.

Casey, D. (1985) 'When is a Team not a Team', *Personnel Management*, January.

Cattell, R.B. and Warburton, F.W. (1967) *Objective Personality and Motivation Tests*, London: University of Illinois Press.

Checkland, P. (1981) *Systems Thinking, Systems Practice*, Chichester: Wiley.

Cohen, A. (1986) *Two Dimensional Man: An Essay on the Anthropology of Power and Symbolism*, London: Routledge and Kegan Paul.

Comte, A. (1853), *The Positive Philosophy of Auguste Comte*, [translated: H. Martineau], London: Trubner & Co.

Converse, J.M. and Previer, S. (1986) *Survey Questions: Handcrafting the Standardised Questionnaire*, Quantitative Applications in the Social Sciences No 63, Beverly Hills: Sage.

Cook, T.D. and Campbell, D.T. (1979) *Quasi-Experimentation: Design and Analysis Issues for Field Settings*, Chicago: Rand McNally.

Critchley, B. and Casey, D. (1984) 'Second Thoughts on Team Building', *Management Education and Development*, 15(2): 163–75.

Curran, J. and Downing, S. (1989) 'The State and Small Business Owners: An Empirical Assessment of Consultation Strategies', paper presented at the 12th National Small Firms Policy and Research Conference, Barbican, London.

Currie, R.M. (1959) *Work Study*, London: Pitman.

Cyert, R.H. and March, J.G. (1963) *A Behavioural History of the Firm*, Englewood-Cliffs NJ: Prentice-Hall.

Dalton, M. (1959) *Men Who Manage: Fusion of Feeling and Theory in Administration*, New York: Wiley.

Dalton, M. (1964) 'Preconceptions and Methods in *Men Who Manage*' in P. Hammond (ed.) *Sociologists at Work*, New York: Basic Books.

Dare, G.A. and Bakewell, K.G.B. (1983) *The Manager's Guide to Getting Answers*, London: Library Association.

Davila, C. (1989) 'Grounding Management Education in Local Research: A Latin American Experience' in J. Davies, M. Easterby-Smith, S. Mann and M. Tanton (eds), *The Challenge to Western Management Development: International Alternatives*, London: Routledge.

De Bono, E. (1971) *Practical Thinking*, London: Jonathan Cape.

Denzin, N.K. (1971) 'The Logic of Naturalistic Inquiry' *Social Forces*, 50: 166–82.

Ditton, J. (1977) *Part-time Crime*, London: Macmillan.

Douglas, J.D. (ed.) (1976) *Investigative Social Research*, Beverly Hills: Sage.

Easterby-Smith, M. (1980) 'How to Use Repertory Grids in HRD', *Journal of European Industrial Training Monograph*, 4(2): 1–32.

Easterby-Smith, M. (1986) *Evaluation of Management Education, Training and Development*, Aldershot: Gower.

Easterby-Smith, M. and Ashton, D. (1975) 'Using Repertory Grid Technique to Evaluate Management Training', *Personnel Review*, 4(4): 15–21.

Eden, C. (1988a) 'Cognitive Mapping as a Visionary Tool: Strategy Embedded in Issue Management', Alfred-Houle Seminar, Faculté des Sciences de l'Administration, Université Lavel, Quebec, March.

Eden, C. (1988b) 'Strategic Decision Support through Computer-based Analysis and Presentation of Cognitive Maps', Alfred-Houle Seminar, Faculté des Sciences de l'Administrtion, Université Lavel, Quebec, March.

Eden, C. and Jones, S. (1984) 'Using Repertory Grid for Problem Construction', *Journal of Operational Research Society*, 35(9): 779–90.

Eden, C. and Radford, J. (eds) (1990), *Tackling Strategic Problems: The Role of Group Decision Support*, London: Sage.

Eden, C., Jones, S. and Sims, D. (1979) *Thinking in Organisations*, London: Macmillan.

Eden, C., Jones, S. and Sims, D. (1983) *Messing About in Problems*, Oxford: Pergamon.

Elbow, P. (1981) *Writing with Power*, Oxford: Oxford University Press.

Evered, R. (1981) 'Management Education for the Year 2000' in C.L. Cooper (ed.), *Developing Managers for the 1980's*, London: Macmillan.

Eysenck, H.J. and Eysenck, S.B.G. (1973) *Eysenck Personality Inventory*, London: University of London Press.

Fairhurst, E. (1983), 'Organisational Rules and the Accomplishment of Nursing Work on Geriatric Wards' in S. Fineman and I. Mangham (eds), 'Qualitative

Approaches to Organisations', *Journal of Management Studies, Special Issue*, 20(3) July: 315–32.

Fineman, S. and Mangham, I. (1983) (eds) 'Qualitative approaches to organisations' *Journal of Management Studies, Special Issue*, 20(3) July: 295–300.

Fayol, H. (1916/50), *Administration Industrielle et Générale*, Paris: Dunod.

Fielding, N.G. (1987) 'The Qualitative Analysis', ESRC Seminar, University of Surrey, September.

Fielding, N.G. and Fielding, J.L. (1986) *Linking Data*, Beverly Hills: Sage.

Finch, J. (1986) *Research and Policy: The Uses of Qualitative Methods in Social and Educational Research*, London: Falmer Press.

Flanagan, J.C. (1954) 'The Critical Incident Technique', *Psychological Bulletin*, 1: 327–58.

French, W.L. and Bell, C.H. Jr. (1978) *Organisation Development: Behavioral Science Interventions for Organisation Improvement*, 2nd ed., Englewood Cliffs, NJ: Prentice-Hall.

Geertz, C. (1973), *The Interpretation of Cultures*, New York: Basic Books.

Glaser, D.G. (1978) *Theoretical Sensitivity*, Mill Valley, California: The Sociological Press.

Glaser, D.G. and Strauss, A.L. (1967) *The Discovery of Grounded Theory: Strategies for Qualitative Research*, New York: Aldine.

Gordon, R.A. and Howell, J.E. (1959) *Higher Education for Business*, New York: Columbia University Press.

Green, P.E. and Tull, D.S. (1978) *Research for Marketing Decisions*, Englewood Cliffs: Prentice-Hall.

Gubrium, J.F. and Silverman, D. (eds) (1989) *The Politics of Field Research*, London: Sage.

Gummesson, E. (1988) *Qualitative Research in Management*, Bromley: Chartwell-Bratt.

Habermas, J. (1970) 'Knowledge and Interest' in D. Emmet and A. MacIntyre (eds), *Sociological Theory and Philosophical Analysis*, London: Macmillan.

Hakin, C. (1987) *Research Design: Strategies and Choices in the Design of Social Research*, London: Allen & Unwin.

Hales, C. (1986) 'What do Managers do? A Critical Review of the Evidence', *Journal of Management Studies*, 23(1) January.

Hall, C.S. (1954) *Primer of Freudian Psychology*, London: Mentor.

Hammersley, M. and Atkinson, P. (1983) *Ethnography: Principles in Practice*, London: Tavistock.

Handy, C. (1978) *Understanding Organisations*, Harmondsworth: Penguin.

Handy, C. (1984) *The Future of Work*, Oxford: Blackwell.

Handy, C., Gordon, C., Gow, I. and Randlesome, C. (1988) *Making Managers*, London: Pitman.

Handy, C. (1989) *The Age of Unreason*, London: Business Books.

Hayes, R.H. and Abernathy, W.J. (1980) 'Managing our Way to Economic Decline', *Harvard Business Review*, 58: 67–77.

Hedges, A. (1985) 'Group Interviewing' in R. Walker (ed.), *Applied Qualitative Research*, Aldershot: Gower.

Herzberg, F., Mausner, B. and Snyderman, B.B. (1959), *The Motivation to Work*, New York: Wiley.

Hickson, D.J. (1988) 'Ruminations on Munificence and Scarcity in Research' in A. Bryman (ed.), *Doing Research in Organisations*, London: Routledge.

Hirschman, E. (1986) 'Humanistic Inquiry in Marketing Research: Philosophy, Method and Criteria', *Journal of Marketing Research*, 23, August: 237–49.

Hofstede, G. (1980; abridged edition, 1984) *Culture's Consequences: International Differences in Work-Related Values*, Beverly Hills: Sage.

Hofstede, G. (1983), 'Culture and Management Development', Geneva: ILO.

Hoinville, G. and Jowell, R. (1978), *Survey Research Practice*, London: Heinemann.

Holmen, M.G. (1979) 'Action Research: the Solution or the Problem?' in C.L. Cooper (ed.) *Behavioral Problems in Organisations*, Englewood Cliffs, NJ: Prentice-Hall.

Hoinville, G. and Jowell, R. (1978), *Survey Research Practice*, London: Heinemann.

Holmen, M.G. (1979) 'Action Research: the Solution or the Problem?' in C.L. Cooper (ed.) *Behavioral Problems in Organisations*, Prentice-Hall.

Holsti, O. (1969) *Content Analysis for the Social Sciences and Humanities*, London: Addison Wesley.

Honey, P. and Mumford, A. (1982) *The Manual of Learning Styles*, published by Peter Honey, Ardingley House, 10, Linden Avenue, Maidenhead, SC6 6HB.

Howard, K. and Sharp, J.A. (1983), *The Management of a Student Research Project*, Aldershot: Gower.

Huff, D. (1973) *How to Lie with Statistics*, Harmondsworth: Penguin.

Husserl, E. (1946) 'Phenomenology' in *Encyclopaedia Britannica*, 14th ed. Vol. 17: 699–702.

Hyder, S. and Sims, D. (1979) 'Hypothesis, Analysis and Paralysis: Issues in the Organisation of Contract Research', *Management Education Development*, 10: 100–11.

Jobber, D. and Horgan, I. (1987) 'Market Research Education: Perspectives from Practitioners', *Journal of Marketing Management*, 3(1): 39–49.

Jones, S. (1985) 'Depth Interviews' in R. Walker, *Applied Qualitative Research*, Aldershot: Gower.

Jones, S. (1985) 'The Analysis of Depth Interviews' in R. Walker, *Applied Qualitative Research*, Aldershot: Gower.

Jones, S. (1987) 'Choosing Action Research: a Rationale' in I.L. Mangham (ed.), *Organisation Analysis and Development*, Chichester: Wiley.

Junkers, B.H. (1960) *Fieldwork: an Introduction to the Social Sciences*, Chicago University Press Cambridge University Press.

Keat, R. (1981) *The Politics of Social Theory*, Oxford: Blackwell.

Kelly, G.A. (1955) *The Psychology of Personal Constructs*, New York: Norton.

Kidder, L.H. and Judd, C.M. (1986) *Research Methods in Social Relations*, London: H.R.W. Intermation.

Kirk, J. and Miller, M.L. (1986), *Reliability and Validity in Qualitative Research*, Beverly Hills: Sage.

Koestler, A. (1964) *The Act of Creation*, London: Hutchinson.

Kolb, D.A. (1984) *Organisational Psychology: An Experiential Approach to Organisational Behaviour*, Englewood Cliffs, NJ: Prentice Hall.

Kolb, D.A. (1986) *Experiential Learning*, Englewood Cliffs, NJ: Prentice-Hall.

Kolb, D.A. and Fry, R. (1975) 'Towards an Applied Theory of Experiential Learning' in C.L. Cooper (ed.), *Theories of Group Processes*, London: Wiley.

Kotter, J. (1982) *The General Managers*. Glencoe, Illinois: Free Press.

Kuhn, T.S. (1962) *The Structure of Scientific Revolutions*, Chicago: University of Chicago Press.

Lavrakas, P.K. (1987) *Telephone Survey Methods*, Sage Applied Social Research Methods Series, Newbury Park, CA: Sage.

Lawrence, P. (1986) *Invitation to Management*, Oxford: Blackwell.

Lawrence, P. (1988), 'In Another Country', in A. Bryman (ed.) *Doing Research in Organisations*, London: Routledge.

Lee, R. and Piper, J.A. (1986) 'How Views about the Nature of Management can Affect the Content of Management Education Programmes', *Management Education and Development*, 17(2): 114–27.

Legge, K. (1984) *Evaluating Planned Organisational Change*, London: Academic Press.

Lincoln, Y.S. and Guba, G. (1986) *Naturalistic Inquiry*, London: Sage.

Livingston, J.S. (1971) 'The Myth of the Well-educated Manager', *Harvard Business Review*, 49: 79–89.

Lofland, J. (1971) *Analysing Social Settings: A Guide to Qualitative Observation and Analysis*, Belmont, CA: Wadsworth.

Lofland, J. (1974), 'Styles of Reporting Qualitative Field Research', *American Sociologist*, 9 (August): 101–11.

Lowe, A. and Nilsson, T. (1989) *The Ideologies of Scottish Lawyers*, Centre for Professional and Legal Studies, University of Strathclyde.

Macfarlane, G. (1985), *Alexander Fleming: The Man and the Myth*, Oxford: Oxford University Press.

Mackinlay, T. (1986) 'The Development of a Personal Strategy of Management'. Master of Science Degree, Manchester Polytechnic, Department of Management.

McClelland, D.A. (1961) *The Achieving Society*, Princetown: Van Nostrand.

McClelland, D.A. (1965) 'Achievement and Enterprise', *Journal of Personal Social Psychology*, 1: 389–92.

Mangham, I.L. (1986) 'In Search of Competence', *Journal of General Management*, 12(2) Winter: 5–12.

Margerison, C. and Lewis, C. (1986) 'Management Educators and their Clients' in J. Beck and C. Cox (eds) *Advances in Management Education*, Chichester: Wiley: 277–82.

Maruyama, M. (1981) 'Endogenous Research: Rationale' in P. Reason and J. Rowan (eds) *Human Inquiry: A Source Book of New Paradigm Research*, Chichester: Wiley.

Maxwell, A.E. (1970) *Basic Statistics in Behavioural Research*, Harmondsworth: Penguin.

Mayo, E. (1949) *The Social Problems of an Industrial Civilisation*, London: Routledge and Kegan Paul.

Mendes de Almeida (1980) 'A Review of Group Discussion Methodology', *European Research*, 8(3): 114–20.

Merton, R.K. and Kendal, P.C. (1957) *The Student Physician*, Cambridge, MA: Harvard University Press.

Miles, N.B. and Huberman, A.M. (1984) *Qualitative Data Analysis: A Sourcebook of New Methods*, London: Sage.

Mill, C.W. (1959) *The Sociological Imagination*, Oxford: Oxford University Press.

Mills, C.W. (1972) 'Language Logic and Culture' in A. Cashadan and E. Crugoen (eds) *Language and Educaton*, London: Routledge and Kegan Paul.

Mintzberg, H. (1973) *The Nature of Managerial Work*, London: Harper and Row.

Mintzberg, H. (1978) 'Mintzberg's Final Paradigm', *Administrative Science Quarterly*, 23(4): 635–6.

Morgan, G. (1979) 'Response to Mintzberg', *Administrative Science Quarterly*, 24(1): 137–9.

Morgan, G. (1986) *Images of Organization*, Beverly Hills: Sage.

Morgan, G. and Smircich, L. (1980) 'The Case for Qualitative Research', *Academy of Management Review*, 5: 491–500.

Moser, C.A. and Kalton, G. (1971), *Survey Methods in Social Investigation*, 2nd ed., London: Heineman.

Mullins, C.J. (1977) *A Guide to Writing and Publishing*, Chichester: Wiley.

Murray, H. (1938) *Explorations in Personality, a Clinical and Experimental Study of 50 men of College Age*, New York: Oxford University Press.

Nichols, G. (1980) 'A Study of the National Coal Board's Productivity Bonus Scheme'. Master of Science Thesis, Strathclyde Business School, Glasgow.

Nisbet, J.D. and Entwistle, N.J. (1984) 'Writing the Report' in J. Bell, T. Bush, A. Fox, J. Goodey and S. Goulding (eds.) *Conducting Small-Scale Investigations in Educational Management*, London: Harper and Row.

Nonaka, I. (1988) 'Toward Middle-up-down Management: Accelerating Information Creation', *Sloan Management Review*, Spring: 9–18.

Norusis, M.. (1986) *The SPSS Guide to Data Analysis*, Chicago: SPSS Inc.

Oppenheim, A.N. (1966) *Questionnaire Design and Attitude Measurement*, London: Heinemann.

Patchen, M. (1965) *Some Questionnaire Measures of Employee Motivation and Morale*, Ann Arbor, Michigan: ISR.

Patton, M.Q. (1980) *Qualitative Evaluation Methods*, London: Sage.

Pears, D. (1971), *Wittgenstein*, London: Fontana.

Peters, T.J. and Waterman, R.H. (1982) *In Search of Excellence: Lessons from America's Best Run Companies*, New York: Harper and Row.

Pettigrew, A.M. (1983) 'On Studying Organisational Cultures', in J. Van Maanan (ed.) *Qualitative Methodology*, London: Sage.

Pettigrew, A.M. (1985) 'Contextualist Research: A Natural Way to Link Theory and Practice' in E.E. Lawler (ed.), *Doing Research that is Useful in Theory and Practice*, San Francisco: Jossey Bass.

Pfaffenberger, B. (1988) *Micro-computer Applications for Qualitative Research*, London: Sage.

Phillips, E.M. (1984) 'Learning to Do Research', *Graduate Management Research*, 2(1): 6–18.

Phillips, E.M. and Pugh, D.S. (1987) *How to Get a PhD*, Milton Keynes: Open University Press.

Platt, J. (1976) *Realities of Social Research: An Empirical Study of British Sociologists*, Brighton: Sussex University Press.

Popper, K. (1959) *The Logic of Scientific Discovery*, London: Hutchinson.

Porter, L.W. and McKibbin, L.E. (1988) *Management Education and Development: Drift or Thrust into the 21st Century?*, New York, McGraw-Hill.

Prince, G.M. (1970) *The Practice of Creativity: A Manual for Group Problem Solving*, London: Harper and Row.

Pugh, D.S. and Hickson, D.J. (1976) *Organisation Structure in its Context: The Aston Programme*, Farnborough: Saxon House.

Pugh, D.S. (1983) 'Studying Organisational Structure and Process' in G. Morgan (ed.), *Beyond Method*, Beverly Hills: Sage.

Pugh, D.S. (1984) 'What is Research' in A. Chapman (ed.) *What Has Management Research Got to Do With Managers?*, London: ATM Focus Paper.

Pugh, D.S. (1988) 'The Aston Research Programme' in A. Bryman (ed.), *Doing Research in Organisations*, London: Routledge.

Punch, M. (1986) *The Politics and Ethics of Fieldwork*, Beverly Hills: Sage.

Reason, P. (1988) *Human Inquiry in Action*, London: Sage.

Revans, R.W. (1971), *Developing Effective Managers*, New York: Appleton Century Crofts.

Reason, P. and Rowan, J. (1981) *Human Inquiry: A Sourcebook of New Paradigm Research*, London: Wiley.

Revans, R.W. (1980) *Action Learning: New Technology for Management*, London: Blond and Briggs.

Revans, R.W. (1982) *The Origins and Growth of Action Learning*, Bromley: Chartwell-Bratt.

Rickards, T. (1988) *Problem Solving Through Creativity at Work*, Aldershot: Gower.

Rogers, C.R. (1967) *On Becoming a Person: A Therapist's View of Psychotherapy*, London: Constable.

Roy, D. (1952), 'Quota Restriction and Goldbricking in a Machine Shop', *American Journal of Sociology*, 57: 427–42.

Roy, D. (1970) 'The Study of Southern Labour Union Organising Campaigns' in R. Haberstein (ed.) *Pathway to Data*, New York: Aldine.

Ryan, B., Joiner, B.L. and Ryan, T.A. (1985) *Student Handbook*, Boston: Duxbury Press.

Ryave, A.L. and Schenkein, J.N. (1974), Notes on the Art of Walking, in R. Turner (ed.) *Ethnomethodology: Selected Readings*, Harmondsworth: Penguin.

Schrudt, P. (1987) *Micro Computer Methods for Social Scientists*, London: Sage.

Selvin, H.C. and Stuart, A. (1966) 'Data-dredging Procedures in Survey Analysis', *American Statistician*, 20: 20–23.

Siegal, S. (1956) *Non-parametric Statistics for the Behavioral Sciences*, New York: McGraw-Hill.

Silverman, D. (1970) *The Theory of Organisations: A Sociological Framework*, London: Heinemann.

Simon, H.A. (1959) *Administrative Behaviour*, 2nd ed. London: Macmillan.

Slater, D. (1989) 'Corridors of Power' in J.F. Gubrium and D. Silverman (eds), *The Politics of Field Research*, London: Sage

Smith, H.W. (1975) *Strategies of Social Research: The Methodological Imagination*, London: Prentice-Hall.

Snell, R.S. (1986) 'Questioning the Ethics of Management Development: A Critical Review', *Management Education and Development*, 17(1): 43–64.

Spender, J. (1980) *Man Made Language*, London: Routledge, Kegan Paul.

Spender, J. (1989) *Industry Recipes: The Nature and Sources of Managerial Judgement*, Oxford: Basil Blackwell.

Steinbeck, J. (1970) *Journal of a Novel: The East of Eden Letters*, London: Pan Books.

Stewart, R. (1967) *Managers and their Jobs*, Maidenhead: McGraw-Hill.

Stewart, R. (1982) *Choices for the Manager: A Guide to Managerial Work and Behaviour*, London: McGraw-Hill.

Stewart, V. and Stewart, A. (1981) *Business Applications of Repertory Grid*, Maidenhead: McGraw-Hill.

Sudman, S. (1976) *Applied Sampling*, London: Academic Press.

Susman, G.I. and Evered, R.D. (1978) 'An Assessment of the Scientific Merits of Action Research', *Administrative Science Quarterly*, 23: 582–603.

Taylor, F.W. (1947) *Scientific Management*, London: Harper and Row.

Taylor, S.J. and Bogdan, R. (1984) *Introduction to Qualitative Research Methods*, New York: Wiley-Interscience.

Thomas, W.I. and Thomas, D.S. (1928) *The Child in America: Behavioural Problems and Progress*, New York: Knopf.

Thomas, B.E. (1988) 'Planning for Performance: the Management of Change in General Medical Services'. Master of Science Degree Dissertation, Manchester Polytechnic.

Thomas, A.B. (1989), 'One Minute Management: A Sign of the Times?', *Management Education and Development*, 20(1): 23–38.

Thorpe, R. (1980), 'The Relationship Between Payment Systems, Productivity and the Organisation of Work', Master of Science Thesis, Strathclyde Business School.

Todd, D.J. (1979) 'Mixing Qualitiative and Quantitative Methods: Triangulation in Action', *Administrative Science Quarterly*, 24, December: 602–11.

Tuck, M. (1976), *How Do We Choose?*, London: Methuen.

Turner, B.A. (1981) 'Quality and Quantity', *Elsevier Scientific Publishing*, Amsterdam, 15: 225–47.

Turner, B.A. (1983) 'The Use of Grounded Theory for the Qualitative Analysis of Organisational Behaviour', *Journal of Management Studies*, 20(3): 333–48.

Turner, B.A. (1987) 'Communications between Supervisor and Postgraduate about Theory'. ESRC Conference, University of Norwich, December.

Turner, B.A. (1988), 'Connoisseurship in the Study of Organisational Cultures', in A. Bryman (ed.) *Doing Research in Organisations*, London: Routledge.

Usunier, J.C. (1986) 'Promouvoir la qualité dans les services pour développer l'emploi, Ecole Superieure de commerce de Paris: No. 86–61.

Van Maanen, J. (1983) *Qualitative Methodology*, London: Sage.

Vidich, A.J. (1954) 'Participant Observation and the Collection and Interpretation of Data', *American Journal of Sociology*, 60: 354–60.

Von Bertalanffy, L. (1962) 'General Systems Theory – a Critical Review', *General Systems* VII: 1–20.

Walker, R. (1985) *Applied Qualitative Research*, Aldershot: Gower.

Walton, M. (1989) *The Deming Management Method*, London: Mercury Books.

White, S.E. and Mitchell, T.R. (1976) 'Organisation Development: A Review of Research Content and Research Design', *Academy of Management Review*, April: 57–73.

Whitley, R., Thomas A. and Marceau, J. (1981) *Masters of Business?* London: Tavistock.

Youngman, M.B. (1984) 'Designing Questionnaires' in J. Bell, T. Bush, A. Fox, J. Goodey and S. Goulding (eds), *Conducting Small-Scale Investigations in Educational Management*, London: Harper and Row.

Index